DEDICATION PAGE

The Holy Spirit

will

guide my steps

While every precaution has been taken in the preparation of this book, the publisher assumes no responsibility for errors or omissions, or for damages resulting from the use of the information contained herein.

GUARDING YOUR HEART

First edition. December 17, 2023.

Copyright © 2023 BGodInspired.

ISBN: 979-8223764588

Written by BGodInspired.

BENEFITS OF SHORT BIBLE STUDY

We provide short, easy-to-consume content with a positive message based on biblical principles. There are several benefits of a short Bible study series, including:

- **Accessibility**: Short Bible study series are more accessible for people with busy schedules who may not have the time to commit to longer studies.

- **Focus**: Short Bible study series allow for a more focused study on a specific topic or theme. This can help participants to gain a deeper understanding of a particular aspect of the Bible.

- **Flexibility**: Short Bible study series can be adapted to suit the needs of different groups or individuals. They can be tailored to fit different schedules, learning styles, and levels of biblical knowledge.

- **Engagement**: Short Bible study series are often more engaging than longer studies because they require less time commitment and allow participants to see progress quickly.

- **Variety**: Short Bible study series can be used to explore different topics and themes, providing a variety of learning experiences for participants.

- **Accountability**: Short Bible study series can create a sense of accountability among participants, who are more likely to complete the study if they know it will only take a few weeks.

Overall, a short Bible study series can be a great way to engage with the Bible in a meaningful way, no matter what your schedule or level of knowledge may be..

Extract the positive aspects that align with you, apply them to your life, enjoy the benefits you receive. :)

TABLE OF CONTENTS

Introduction: Guarding Your Heart - A Biblical Devotional

The heart stands as a profound symbol—a repository of our emotions, thoughts, and intentions. It's the epicenter of our being, the wellspring from which the waters of life flow. From its chambers arise the love that shapes our relationships, the dreams that guide our endeavors, and the desires that fuel our actions. But as with any precious vessel, the heart is vulnerable to both beauty and blemish.

The Bible, a timeless repository of wisdom and truth, beckons us to heed the ancient call to "guard your heart, for everything you do flows from it" (Proverbs 4:23, NIV). This devotional embarks on a journey into the heart—a journey rooted in the rich soil of Scripture and guided by the light of faith. In the following pages, we will delve into the profound teachings of the Bible and uncover the profound art of guarding the heart.

Amidst the clamor of the world and the ever-shifting sands of circumstance, this devotional serves as a lighthouse—a steady beam that directs our gaze inward, towards the center of our being. It's an invitation to consider the significance of guarding our hearts, not as an isolated endeavor, but as a vital aspect of our relationship with the Creator.

As we explore the biblical principles and stories woven into the fabric of guarding the heart, may we find encouragement, challenge, and renewal. In the heart's guarding, we discover a pathway to spiritual growth, resilience, and a deeper intimacy with God. It's an ongoing process, an endeavor that requires vigilance, yet promises immeasurable reward.

So, let us embark on this journey together—delving into the wisdom of Scripture, examining the challenges of the human heart, and embracing the transformative power of a heart aligned with God's truth. As we learn to guard our hearts, may we find the courage to navigate life's currents with grace, to nurture relationships with wisdom, and to pursue our divine purpose with unwavering devotion.

In each chapter, we will unravel a different facet of guarding the heart, inviting you to reflect, ponder, and apply these truths to your own life. Let the pages that follow be a sanctuary—a place of contemplation, growth, and connection with the One who intricately designed our hearts and calls us to steward them well.

Chapter 1: The Source of Life

"Above all else, guard your heart, for everything you do flows from it." - Proverbs 4:23 (NIV)

In the tapestry of our existence, the heart holds a place of unmatched significance. It is not merely a biological pump, but a wellspring of life's deepest currents—the epicenter of our thoughts, emotions, and intentions. As we embark on this journey to explore the concept of guarding the heart, we must first uncover the profound role it plays as the source of life.

1.1 The Heart's Remarkable Role

In the vast landscape of human experience, the heart stands as a remarkable and multifaceted entity. It is more than a mere anatomical organ; it is the metaphoric epicenter of our thoughts, emotions, and intentions. Throughout the pages of Scripture, the heart is depicted as the very core of our being—a place of encounter, transformation, and revelation.

In biblical language, the heart embodies the depth of our inner life. It encompasses not just emotion, but also the seat of our will, desires, and decisions. It's the place where we engage with God and wrestle with our deepest questions. When we read verses like Proverbs 27:19 (NIV), which says, "As water reflects the face, so one's life reflects the heart," we are reminded that our hearts are like mirrors reflecting the essence of who we are.

Throughout Jesus' teachings, the heart takes center stage. He emphasized that what emerges from our hearts—our words and actions—defines our character and shapes our interactions. In Matthew 15:18-19 (NIV), Jesus explains, "But the things that come out of a person's mouth come from the heart, and these defile them.

For out of the heart come evil thoughts—murder, adultery, sexual immorality, theft, false testimony, slander."

Yet, the heart is not just a repository of human inclinations. It's also the arena where we can encounter the divine. In Psalm 119:11 (NIV), the psalmist declares, "I have hidden your word in my heart that I might not sin against you." This illustrates the heart's capacity to be a dwelling place for God's truth and presence. When we internalize God's Word, it takes root within our hearts, shaping our thoughts and guiding our actions.

In the New Testament, Jesus further illuminates the heart's potential as a dwelling for the Holy Spirit. In John 14:23 (NIV), He promises, "Anyone who loves me will obey my teaching. My Father will love them, and we will come to them and make our home with them." This intimate dwelling of God within the heart transforms it into a sanctuary—a place of communion, conviction, and divine revelation.

Considering the heart's significance, it becomes clear why guarding it is of paramount importance. Our thoughts, emotions, and intentions flow from the heart, influencing every aspect of our lives. Just as a wellspring's purity determines the quality of its waters, the condition of our hearts determines the quality of our thoughts, actions, and relationships.

As we delve deeper into the journey of guarding our hearts, we will uncover the strategies and insights that Scripture offers. Each chapter will guide us in navigating the complexities of life while staying attuned to the heart's rhythms. By nurturing a heart aligned with God's truth, we create a foundation for a purposeful, intentional, and joy-filled existence.

In the chapters to come, we will explore the vulnerabilities of the heart, its susceptibility to deception, and the transformative power of renewal. We will uncover the beauty of cultivating godly desires, the impact of positive influences, and the significance of community in our heart-guarding journey. As we progress, may we remember that the heart's remarkable role is not just a metaphysical concept, but a tangible force shaping the trajectory of our lives.

1.2 The Fallen Nature of the Heart

As we continue our exploration into the heart's profound role, we encounter a sobering reality—the fallen nature of humanity and its impact on the heart. In the midst of its remarkable potential, the heart is susceptible to the corrosive effects of sin and brokenness, a reality that calls for vigilance and intentional guarding.

Jeremiah 17:9 (NIV) paints a stark picture of the heart's condition: "The heart is deceitful above all things and beyond cure. Who can understand it?" This candid portrayal doesn't deny the heart's depth and complexity, but it acknowledges the inclination of the heart to veer off course. Like a compass with a faulty needle, our hearts can lead us astray, fostering desires and intentions that are far from God's design.

The narrative of humanity's first disobedience in the Garden of Eden illustrates this fallen nature. Adam and Eve's hearts were initially aligned with God's purpose, yet they succumbed to the deception of their own desires and the serpent's cunning. This original sin marred the purity of the heart, introducing a rift between humanity and God.

Paul, in his letter to the Romans, articulates the internal struggle caused by the fallen nature of the heart. He writes in Romans 7:21-23 (NIV), "So I find this law at work: Although I want to do good, evil is right there with me. For in my inner being I delight in God's law; but I see another law at work in me, waging war against the law of my mind and making me a prisoner of the law of sin at work within me."

This passage speaks to the dichotomy within us—a tension between the yearnings of the heart for righteousness and the pull of sin's allure. It echoes the struggle between our God-given potential and the brokenness that has infiltrated our hearts.

Recognizing the fallen nature of the heart is not an invitation to despair, but a call to transformation. While the heart may be deceitful, it is not beyond redemption. The restorative power of God's grace and the indwelling of the Holy Spirit provide a means for heart transformation.

Paul continues in Romans 12:2 (NIV), "Do not conform to the pattern of this world, but be transformed by the renewing of your mind." This transformation—a renewing of the heart—requires a partnership between human effort and divine intervention. By aligning our hearts with God's Word, submitting to His leading, and allowing His Spirit to reshape our desires, we embark on a journey of heart renewal.

As we navigate the intricate landscape of guarding the heart, understanding its fallen nature equips us to approach the task with humility and dependence on God's grace. Our heart-guarding journey is not a solitary endeavor but a response to God's invitation to partake in our own spiritual renewal. The chapters ahead will guide us through the practical ways we can foster this renewal and embrace the abundant life that God desires for us.

1.3 Nurturing a Healthy Heart

In the grand symphony of our existence, the heart plays a pivotal role as both conductor and instrument. It orchestrates the melodies of our emotions, thoughts, and intentions, and it responds to the conductor's baton—the choices we make and the influences we allow. As we continue our exploration, we venture into the art of nurturing a healthy heart, fostering a space where God's purpose can flourish.

Imagine your heart as a garden—an intricate landscape teeming with the potential for vibrant growth. Just as a gardener tends to each plant's needs to ensure their health, we must tend to our hearts with intentionality and care. Proverbs 4:23 (NIV) instructs us to "Above all else, guard your heart, for everything you do flows from it." This admonition underscores the heart's centrality in shaping our lives.

Nurturing a healthy heart involves cultivating godly desires, aligning our intentions with God's will, and creating an environment where His truth can take root. Just as a gardener selects seeds that yield fruit and flowers, we are called to intentionally plant the seeds of God's Word, prayer, and worship within our hearts.

Godly desires stem from an intimate relationship with the Creator. Psalm 37:4 (NIV) affirms, "Take delight in the Lord, and he will give you the desires of your heart." As we draw near to God, our desires begin to align with His heart, reshaping our ambitions and priorities. In this alignment, we find that our yearnings are no longer centered solely on personal gain, but on the advancement of God's kingdom and the well-being of others.

Nurturing godly desires involves intentionally exposing ourselves to God's Word and allowing it to influence our thoughts, ambitions, and choices. Regularly engaging with Scripture helps us recalibrate our hearts, tuning them to the frequency of heaven's desires.

Gratitude is a powerful tool in nurturing a healthy heart. It redirects our focus from what we lack to what we've been given. Colossians 3:15 (NIV) encourages us to "Let the peace of Christ rule in your hearts, since as members of one body you were called to peace. And be thankful." Gratitude not only transforms our perspective but also guards against discontentment and self-centeredness.

Incorporating gratitude into our daily lives becomes an act of spiritual discipline. By keeping a gratitude journal, reflecting on God's blessings, and offering thanks in prayer, we cultivate a heart that acknowledges and appreciates the goodness of God.

Nurturing a healthy heart is a transformative journey—a process of intentional surrender and partnership with God. Through prayer, meditation, and reflection on Scripture, we open ourselves to God's pruning, weeding out the negativity and cultivating the fertile soil of our hearts.

As we delve into the chapters that follow, we will uncover practical strategies for nurturing a healthy heart. We will explore the impact of positive influences, the significance of community, and the art of discerning deception. Let us approach this journey with anticipation, knowing that a well-nurtured heart becomes a vessel for God's love, purpose, and transformative power.

Chapter 2: The Battle for the Heart

"For our struggle is not against flesh and blood, but against the rulers, against the authorities, against the powers of this dark world and against the spiritual forces of evil in the heavenly realms." - Ephesians 6:12 (NIV)

In the realm of the heart, a fierce battle rages—an unseen conflict that extends beyond the physical world. This chapter unveils the spiritual battle that unfolds within the depths of our hearts and explores the crucial role of guarding against negative influences and spiritual attacks.

2.1 The Unseen Battle

In the tapestry of human existence, the heart stands as a battlefield where forces both seen and unseen collide. Ephesians 6:12 vividly portrays this reality: "For our struggle is not against flesh and blood, but against the rulers, against the authorities, against the powers of this dark world and against the spiritual forces of evil in the heavenly realms." This unseen battle—often relegated to the spiritual realm—holds profound implications for the course of our lives.

Our hearts are not neutral territories; they are contested ground in a cosmic conflict between light and darkness. Just as earthly territories are coveted by competing powers, our hearts are sought after by spiritual forces that influence our thoughts, emotions, and actions. These unseen powers operate beyond the physical, orchestrating a tug-of-war for our allegiance.

While the battle may be invisible, its effects are palpable. The inner turmoil, doubts, and struggles we experience are often manifestations of this spiritual clash. The heart becomes the focal point where heavenly and demonic forces vie for supremacy.

Understanding the unseen battle compels us to equip ourselves with spiritual armor. Ephesians 6:13-17 provides a vivid illustration of this armor: the belt of truth, the breastplate of righteousness, the shoes of the gospel of peace, the shield of faith, the helmet of salvation, and the sword of the Spirit (God's Word). This armor, provided by God, empowers us to withstand the enemy's assaults and stand firm.

The armor of God is not a mere metaphor but a symbol of the divine resources available to us. Truth safeguards our minds against deception; righteousness guards our hearts from contamination; faith deflects doubt; salvation secures our identity; the Word of God acts as a weapon against falsehood. Clad in this armor, we enter the battlefield with confidence, knowing that we are equipped for victory.

Guarding the heart in the midst of this battle requires active vigilance. Just as a watchman keeps watch over a city's walls, we must keep watch over the gates of our hearts. Proverbs 4:23 (NIV) emphasizes this responsibility: "Above all else, guard your heart, for everything you do flows from it." Our actions, words, and decisions flow from the condition of our hearts. When we guard our hearts, we impact every facet of our lives.

A vigilant heart is one that is fortified by prayer, steeped in God's Word, and sensitive to the Holy Spirit's leading. It's a heart that recognizes the gravity of the unseen battle and remains unwavering in its devotion to God. This vigilance is not rooted in fear but in a deep trust in God's strength and guidance.

As we navigate the unseen battle, let us remember that our victory is not based on our own strength but on the triumph of Christ. Through His sacrifice, He secured our deliverance from the power of darkness and granted us access to the armor and resources needed to withstand the enemy's attacks.

In this chapter, we've unveiled the unseen battle that rages within our hearts. The subsequent chapters will guide us in practical ways to guard our hearts against the enemy's advances. By embracing the reality of this battle and drawing upon God's strength, we can stand firm and emerge victorious in the ongoing struggle for the heart's allegiance.

2.2 Guarding Against Deception

In the intricate dance of the heart's battleground, one of the enemy's most potent weapons is deception. Just as a skilled strategist uses misinformation to confuse and conquer, spiritual forces manipulate truth to lead hearts astray. As we delve into the tactics of this battle, we must recognize the vital importance of guarding against deception.

Deception is a cunning adversary that preys upon our vulnerabilities. It appeals to our desires, our doubts, and our uncertainties, creating an illusion of truth. In the garden of Eden, the serpent's crafty manipulation led Adam and Eve astray, distorting their perception of God's intentions.

This art of deception continues today. False teachings, distorted ideologies, and half-truths can subtly infiltrate our minds, gradually eroding our understanding of God's Word and His character. Just as a city's defenses are compromised from within, our hearts can be swayed by deceptive influences that undermine our faith.

Discernment is the weapon that pierces through the veil of deception. By grounding ourselves in the unchanging truth of God's Word, we gain the ability to recognize falsehood. Hebrews 4:12 (NIV) describes the Word of God as "alive and active. Sharper than any double-edged sword, it penetrates even to dividing soul and spirit, joints and marrow; it judges the thoughts and attitudes of the heart."

As we meditate on Scripture, we cultivate spiritual discernment that enables us to distinguish between genuine and counterfeit teachings.

By engaging in regular study and seeking the guidance of the Holy Spirit, we develop a defense against the subtleties of deception.

Scripture encourages us to test every spirit and teaching to discern their origin and alignment with God's truth. In 1 John 4:1 (NIV), we are instructed, "Dear friends, do not believe every spirit, but test the spirits to see whether they are from God, because many false prophets have gone out into the world." This directive reminds us of the responsibility to evaluate the messages that shape our beliefs.

In the midst of an information-saturated world, we must engage our critical thinking skills and the discernment provided by the Holy Spirit. Evaluating teachings, ideologies, and influences against the yardstick of Scripture helps us guard our hearts against deceptive currents.

Guarding against deception is closely tied to the renewal of the mind. Romans 12:2 (NIV) urges us, "Do not conform to the pattern of this world, but be transformed by the renewing of your mind. Then you will be able to test and approve what God's will is—his good, pleasing and perfect will." A renewed mind is fortified against deception, able to discern God's will even in the midst of confusion.

In this ongoing battle, nurturing a heart that is rooted in the truth of God's Word is paramount. By staying vigilant against deception and cultivating a discerning heart, we equip ourselves to navigate the currents of misinformation and emerge victorious in our pursuit of guarding the heart.

2.3 Resisting Temptation

In the theater of the heart's battleground, temptation emerges as a formidable opponent—a force that seeks to lure us away from God's purpose and entangle us in the web of compromise. As we delve into the intricacies of this battle, we must grasp the significance of resisting temptation and standing firm against its advances.

Temptation is the subtle invitation to satisfy our desires in ways that deviate from God's design. It exploits our vulnerabilities, leveraging our human inclinations for pleasure, power, or security. Just as a skillful fisherman uses an enticing bait to catch fish, temptation lures us with promises of fulfillment while concealing the destructive hook that lies beneath.

The roots of temptation trace back to the Garden of Eden, where the serpent enticed Eve with the forbidden fruit. The enemy's tactics haven't changed; he continues to manipulate our desires to lead us away from God's path.

The Gospel accounts of Jesus' temptations in the wilderness (Matthew 4:1-11) provide a blueprint for resisting temptation. In this encounter, the enemy targeted Jesus' physical needs, His desire for recognition, and His commitment to God's will. Jesus countered each temptation with the Word of God, demonstrating the power of Scripture in repelling the enemy's advances.

This narrative illustrates that resisting temptation involves more than sheer willpower—it requires a deep connection with God's Word and an unwavering commitment to obedience. By internalizing God's truth, we fortify our hearts against the allure of temptation.

Resisting temptation requires building spiritual resilience—a steadfast foundation that withstands the storms of desire and the enemy's attacks. Psalm 119:11 (NIV) declares, "I have hidden your word in my heart that I might not sin against you." By immersing ourselves in Scripture, we cultivate a reservoir of truth that bolsters our resistance against temptation.

Prayer also plays a pivotal role in fortifying our hearts. Jesus' instruction to His disciples in the Garden of Gethsemane (Matthew 26:41) underscores the significance of prayer in overcoming temptation:

"Watch and pray so that you will not fall into temptation. The spirit is willing, but the flesh is weak." In prayer, we draw upon God's strength to navigate the internal conflict between our desires and our commitment to righteousness.

In the heart's battle against temptation, accountability serves as a crucial ally. Proverbs 27:17 (NIV) affirms, "As iron sharpens iron, so one person sharpens another." Sharing our struggles and seeking support from fellow believers can provide a safe space for transparency and growth. Accountability partners can offer encouragement, prayer, and practical advice, helping us navigate the treacherous waters of temptation.

In this ongoing battle, the goal is not to eliminate the existence of temptation but to equip ourselves to respond effectively when it arises. By immersing ourselves in God's Word, fostering a lifestyle of prayer, and seeking accountability, we develop a robust defense against the allure of temptation. With our hearts rooted in God's truth, we are better equipped to stand firm and emerge victorious in the battle for the heart.

2.4 The Role of Prayer

In the heart's battleground, prayer emerges as a powerful weapon—a means of communication with the divine Commander who guides our every move. As we navigate the complexities of this battle, we must recognize the integral role of prayer in guarding our hearts, seeking divine guidance, and finding strength in the face of challenges.

Prayer is not merely a religious duty; it is a privilege—a direct line of communication with the Creator of the universe. Just as a soldier relies on communication with their commander, we depend on prayer to commune with God, our ultimate Source of wisdom and strength.

Through prayer, we lay bare our concerns, aspirations, and struggles, inviting God's intervention into the intricate tapestry of our hearts.

In prayer, we acknowledge our dependence on God's guidance and acknowledge that the battles we face are not ours alone. We surrender control and open ourselves to His leading, trusting that He will equip us for the challenges that lie ahead.

Prayer is not passive; it's an active engagement in spiritual warfare. Ephesians 6:18 (NIV) emphasizes this by urging believers to "pray in the Spirit on all occasions with all kinds of prayers and requests. With this in mind, be alert and always keep on praying for all the Lord's people." Prayer is the battlefield where we counteract the enemy's advances and align ourselves with God's purposes.

Just as a commander strategizes and coordinates troops in a battle, prayer aligns our hearts with God's strategies. In prayer, we can intercede for ourselves and others, rebuke spiritual opposition, and seek divine wisdom to discern the enemy's tactics. By making prayer a constant practice, we ensure that our hearts remain fortified against the enemy's assaults.

Prayer not only empowers us but also strengthens us in times of weakness. In our battles against temptation, doubt, and adversity, we can draw upon God's strength through prayer. Jesus' prayer in the Garden of Gethsemane exemplifies this principle. Facing the weight of the cross, He prayed for strength, expressing His willingness to submit to God's will (Matthew 26:36-46).

In our moments of vulnerability, prayer becomes a refuge—a place of solace and renewal. By lifting our concerns to God, we find assurance that He is our ever-present help in times of trouble (Psalm 46:1). Prayer allows us to surrender our weaknesses to the One who is our source of strength.

Cultivating the role of prayer in guarding the heart involves embracing it as a lifestyle, not just a ritual. The apostle Paul's exhortation in 1 Thessalonians 5:17 (NIV) encapsulates this: "pray continually." A lifestyle of prayer involves a constant connection with God—seeking His guidance in daily decisions, offering gratitude for His blessings, and seeking His wisdom in moments of uncertainty.

As we journey through the battleground of the heart, may we remember that prayer is our lifeline—a channel through which we connect with the One who equips us for victory. By fostering a vibrant prayer life, we invite God's presence into every aspect of our journey, ensuring that our hearts remain guarded, attuned, and prepared for the challenges that lie ahead.

2.5 The Victory of the Heart

In the heart's battlefield, victory is not a distant possibility—it is a reality that unfolds as we align our hearts with God's purposes and wield the spiritual weapons at our disposal. As we delve into the culmination of this battle, we discover the triumphant culmination of guarding the heart—a victory that transforms us from within and radiates outward.

The battle for the heart is not fought in vain; it is a transformative journey that shapes our character, refines our desires, and deepens our intimacy with God. Romans 12:2 (NIV) encapsulates this transformation: "Do not conform to the pattern of this world, but be transformed by the renewing of your mind. Then you will be able to test and approve what God's will is—his good, pleasing and perfect will." Guarding the heart involves aligning our desires with God's truth, allowing our minds to be renewed, and embracing His will as our own.

This transformation is not a one-time event, but an ongoing process—a journey that extends beyond the battle's conclusion. Just as a warrior's training doesn't end with a single victory, our pursuit of guarding the heart continues as we navigate life's complexities and grow in spiritual maturity.

The victory of the heart doesn't merely result in survival; it leads to abundant living. Jesus declared in John 10:10 (NIV), "I have come that they may have life, and have it to the full." When we guard our hearts, we open ourselves to the abundant life that God desires for us. Our relationships become more meaningful, our decisions are guided by wisdom, and our actions reflect Christ's love.

An abundant heart is characterized by joy, contentment, and a deep sense of purpose. It transcends external circumstances and remains anchored in the unchanging truth of God's Word. By guarding our hearts, we cultivate an environment where the fruits of the Spirit—love, joy, peace, patience, kindness, goodness, faithfulness, gentleness, and self-control—flourish.

The victory of the heart extends beyond personal transformation—it radiates influence to those around us. Just as a lighthouse's beacon guides ships to safety, our transformed hearts illuminate the path for others to find hope, healing, and purpose in Christ. Matthew 5:16 (NIV) captures this idea: "In the same way, let your light shine before others, that they may see your good deeds and glorify your Father in heaven."

When our hearts are guarded and transformed, our lives become a testament to God's transformative power. Our actions, words, and attitudes draw others into the beauty of a life lived in alignment with God's truth. By intentionally guarding our hearts, we become vessels through which God's love and grace flow to a world in need.

Ultimately, the victory of the heart carries an eternal perspective. While battles may rage in the present, Scripture assures us of a future where

God's victory is fully realized. Revelation 21:4 (NIV) paints a glimpse of this eternal victory: "He will wipe every tear from their eyes. There will be no more death or mourning or crying or pain, for the old order of things has passed away."

The battles we face in guarding the heart are but a prelude to the ultimate victory that awaits us. In the midst of life's challenges, our hearts are anchored in the hope of Christ's return and the promise of a restored and victorious eternity.

As we conclude this chapter, let us remember that the victory of the heart is not a distant dream—it is a present reality that transforms us from the inside out. By guarding our hearts, we embrace the abundant life God offers, radiate His influence to others, and align ourselves with His eternal purposes.

Chapter 3: Cultivating Godly Desires

"Take delight in the Lord, and he will give you the desires of your heart." - Psalm 37:4 (NIV)

Within the terrain of the heart's battleground, desires emerge as powerful influencers, shaping our motivations and decisions. This chapter delves into the art of cultivating godly desires—a transformative journey that aligns our heart's yearnings with God's purposes and leads us to a life of fulfillment and purpose.

3.1 The Power of Desires

Desires are the driving force behind human actions and decisions, shaping the trajectory of our lives. They are the underlying currents that influence our thoughts, emotions, and behaviors, often determining the paths we choose to walk. In this chapter, we explore the profound power of desires and how cultivating godly desires can lead to transformative change.

Desires are the inner compass that guides our journey. Whether simple or complex, they motivate us to pursue various goals, aspirations, and pleasures. Desires can range from the basic need for sustenance and comfort to more intricate longings for success, love, significance, and purpose.

However, desires are not neutral; they possess the potential for both positive and negative outcomes. They can drive us toward selflessness, compassion, and service, or they can lead us down paths of selfishness, greed, and destruction. Recognizing the power inherent in our desires is essential to understanding their role in shaping our lives.

Cultivating godly desires involves aligning our heart's desires with God's purposes and values. Just as a skilled sailor adjusts the sails to catch the wind's direction, we must adjust our desires to catch the currents of God's will. This alignment is crucial because desires, when out of sync with God's design, can lead us astray.

James 4:3 (NIV) sheds light on this: "When you ask, you do not receive, because you ask with wrong motives, that you may spend what you get on your pleasures." When our desires are rooted in self-centeredness, they can hinder our spiritual growth and distance us from God's blessings. Cultivating godly desires ensures that our desires are attuned to God's heart and His plans for our lives.

Desires, when aligned with God's will, become catalysts for transformation. They motivate us to seek God's guidance, engage in spiritual growth, and live lives characterized by righteousness and love. When our desires are transformed, they lead us to actions that bring honor to God and benefit to others.

Cultivating godly desires requires an ongoing relationship with God. As we spend time in His presence, our desires are reshaped by His truth and wisdom. Psalm 37:4 (NIV) captures this principle: "Take delight in the Lord, and he will give you the desires of your heart." When we delight in God, our desires begin to harmonize with His desires for us.

Guarding and nurturing godly desires involves evaluating our motives, surrendering our desires to God's scrutiny, and inviting Him to reshape them. It also requires discernment and a willingness to let go of desires that do not align with His will. By immersing ourselves in Scripture, we gain insight into what God desires for our lives and how our desires can be transformed to reflect His goodness.

Cultivating godly desires is a lifelong journey that requires intentionality and humility. As we invite God into the realm of our desires, we open ourselves to His transformative power. By continually seeking His guidance, our desires become vehicles that drive us closer to Him and bring about positive change in our lives and the lives of others.

3.2 Delighting in the Lord

At the heart of cultivating godly desires lies a transformative principle: delighting in the Lord. This practice doesn't just involve an external show of devotion; it encompasses a deep, intimate connection with God that shapes the desires of our hearts. By delighting in the Lord, we align our yearnings with His purposes, transforming our desires into reflections of His character.

To delight in the Lord is to find joy, satisfaction, and fulfillment in Him above all else. It's a recognition that God is the source of ultimate joy and the One who satisfies the deepest longings of our hearts. Psalm 16:11 (NIV) encapsulates this truth: "You make known to me the path of life; you will fill me with joy in your presence, with eternal pleasures at your right hand."

Delighting in the Lord isn't a mere duty; it's an invitation to experience the richness of God's presence and love. It's an acknowledgment that our desires find their true purpose and fulfillment when anchored in Him.

When we delight in the Lord, our desires undergo a transformative process. As we draw near to Him through prayer, worship, and meditating on His Word, our hearts become attuned to His nature and will. Our desires shift from self-centered pursuits to aspirations that honor God and benefit others.

Cultivating godly desires starts with cultivating a vibrant relationship with God. Through spending time with Him, our hearts become sensitive to His leading and direction. We begin to desire what He desires, valuing the things that align with His kingdom and eternal purposes.

Delighting in the Lord also involves recognizing that He delights in us. Zephaniah 3:17 (NIV) beautifully illustrates God's delight: "The Lord your God is with you, the Mighty Warrior who saves. He will take great delight in you; in his love he will no longer rebuke you, but will rejoice over you with singing."

When we grasp God's delight in us, it transforms our self-perception. We no longer need to seek validation or fulfillment in fleeting desires; instead, we find our identity and worth in God's unconditional love. This realization reshapes our desires, leading us to yearn for a deeper connection with Him rather than seeking fulfillment in the temporary.

Delighting in the Lord is a deliberate practice. It involves carving out intentional moments to be in His presence, to reflect on His goodness, and to seek His will. These practices can include daily prayer, immersing ourselves in Scripture, participating in worship, and cultivating a heart of gratitude.

By consistently delighting in the Lord, we create an environment where godly desires flourish. Our hearts become fertile ground for the transformation of desires that are pleasing to God and in alignment with His plans for us.

Cultivating godly desires through delight is a journey of transformation. As we seek to find our joy and satisfaction in God, our desires are refined, realigned, and renewed. This transformation is not only an internal process; it radiates outward, influencing the choices we make, the relationships we nurture, and the impact we have on the world.

As we continue on this journey, may we embrace the transformative power of delighting in the Lord. By anchoring our desires in His presence and purpose, we create a foundation that leads us toward a life marked by fulfillment, purpose, and a heart aligned with God's eternal desires.

3.3 A Renewed Perspective

In the landscape of the heart's battleground, perspective acts as a compass, guiding the course of our desires and decisions. Cultivating godly desires involves more than just aligning our desires with God's will—it necessitates a complete renewal of our perspective, allowing us to see the world through the lens of God's truth and eternity.

A renewed perspective begins with viewing life through the lens of eternity. In the midst of temporal pursuits and challenges, we're reminded of the eternal perspective provided by 2 Corinthians 4:18 (NIV): "So we fix our eyes not on what is seen, but on what is unseen, since what is seen is temporary, but what is unseen is eternal."

This perspective shifts our focus from the fleeting to the enduring. It helps us discern whether our desires are aligned with the eternal values of God's kingdom or whether they're centered on transient pleasures and accomplishments.

A renewed perspective aligns our priorities with God's eternal values. Jesus emphasized this perspective when He said, "But seek first his kingdom and his righteousness, and all these things will be given to you as well" (Matthew 6:33, NIV). When God's kingdom becomes our primary focus, our desires are shaped by His purposes.

This renewed perspective prompts us to evaluate our desires in light of their eternal impact. Are our desires contributing to the advancement of God's kingdom and the well-being of others? Or are they confined to self-centered pursuits that hold no eternal significance?

A renewed perspective encompasses the value of contentment, recognizing that true fulfillment rests in God alone. Paul's words in

Philippians 4:12-13 (NIV) capture this essence: "I have learned the secret of being content in any and every situation, whether well fed or hungry, whether living in plenty or in want. I can do all this through him who gives me strength."

Contentment guards against desires fueled by envy, comparison, and discontentment. It allows us to appreciate the blessings we have and to avoid the never-ending pursuit of material possessions or fleeting achievements. A renewed perspective prompts us to seek contentment in God's presence rather than in the world's allurements.

Romans 12:2 (NIV) urges us to "be transformed by the renewing of your mind." A renewed perspective involves the transformation of our thought patterns, allowing God's truth to reshape the way we view ourselves, others, and the world around us. It involves dismantling worldly thinking and replacing it with the wisdom found in God's Word.

Through meditation on Scripture, prayer, and reflection, we engage in the process of renewing our minds. As our minds are transformed, our desires naturally follow suit. Desires that once centered on selfish gain and worldly achievements are now aligned with the eternal purpose God has for us.

Cultivating a renewed perspective is an ongoing journey—a continuous effort to see the world as God sees it and to align our desires with His eternal plans. By deliberately choosing to fix our gaze on the eternal, we create a foundation for godly desires that bring lasting fulfillment and contribute to the advancement of God's kingdom.

As we navigate the heart's battleground, let us remember that a renewed perspective goes beyond momentary desires; it transforms the very fabric of our being, shaping our thoughts, motives, and actions in ways that honor God and impact eternity.

3.4 The Role of Contentment

Amidst the clamor of desires within the heart's battlefield, contentment emerges as a powerful force—a stabilizing anchor that guards against the relentless pursuit of temporary satisfactions. In the journey of cultivating godly desires, understanding and practicing contentment is paramount to finding lasting fulfillment and aligning our desires with God's purposes.

Contentment is a state of inner satisfaction that transcends external circumstances. It's the ability to find peace and joy regardless of one's situation. Philippians 4:11-12 (NIV) beautifully captures the essence of contentment: "I have learned to be content whatever the circumstances. I know what it is to be in need, and I know what it is to have plenty."

Contentment is not complacency or resignation; it's a deliberate choice to be grateful for what we have, trusting in God's provision, and recognizing that our ultimate fulfillment rests in Him alone.

In the heart's battleground, greed and envy often drive the pursuit of desires. Greed craves more and more, seeking to accumulate wealth, possessions, and status. Envy covets what others have, fostering discontentment and comparison. Both these forces are counterproductive to cultivating godly desires.

Contentment acts as a barrier against the toxic influences of greed and envy. When we are content with what we have, we're less likely to be consumed by the insatiable hunger for more. Contentment disarms envy, allowing us to rejoice in the blessings of others rather than coveting what they possess.

Contentment involves embracing God's provision in our lives. Hebrews 13:5 (NIV) reminds us, "Keep your lives free from the love of money and be content with what you have, because God has said,

'Never will I leave you; never will I forsake you.'" Contentment grows from the assurance that God is our provider and sustainer, and His love is far more valuable than any material possession.

This perspective enables us to focus on the riches of a relationship with God rather than the accumulation of worldly possessions. When our hearts find contentment in God's presence, the allure of material desires loses its grip.

Contentment is closely linked to adopting a stewardship mindset—a recognition that everything we have is ultimately entrusted to us by God. We are stewards of His resources, and our desires should be aligned with His purposes. Luke 16:10 (NIV) emphasizes this principle: "Whoever can be trusted with very little can also be trusted with much."

A content heart acknowledges that our possessions, talents, and opportunities are gifts from God. This perspective guides our desires toward using these resources for His glory and the well-being of others.

Contentment paves the way for cultivating godly desires by filtering out the desires driven by selfish ambition and discontentment. It allows us to evaluate our desires in the light of God's purposes and eternal values. Through contentment, we become attuned to desires that honor God, contribute to His kingdom, and reflect His character.

As we navigate the heart's battleground, let us remember that contentment doesn't stifle ambition or growth; rather, it guides our desires toward meaningful pursuits that align with God's will. By practicing contentment, we create a fertile soil for cultivating desires that bring joy, purpose, and a deeper connection with God.

3.5 The Journey of Transformation

In the heart's battleground, the cultivation of godly desires is not a one-time event but a transformative journey—a process that reshapes our innermost longings, redirects our ambitions, and leads us to a life marked by purpose, alignment with God's will, and lasting fulfillment. This journey of transformation spans across our thoughts, emotions, and actions, guiding us toward desires that honor God and bring positive change to our lives and the lives of others.

The journey of transforming desires is dynamic and continuous. Just as a garden requires ongoing care to flourish, cultivating godly desires demands a consistent commitment to nurturing our hearts and minds. This process involves a partnership between our willingness and God's transformative power.

As we embark on this journey, we recognize that we're not alone. Philippians 2:13 (NIV) reminds us, "for it is God who works in you to will and to act in order to fulfill his good purpose." God is actively involved in the transformation of our desires, empowering us to align our will with His and bringing about lasting change.

The journey of transformation begins with surrender—a willingness to release our desires to God's scrutiny and align our hearts with His will. Surrender involves humility, acknowledging that God's plans and purposes are higher than our own. Proverbs 16:3 (NIV) captures this principle: "Commit to the Lord whatever you do, and he will establish your plans."

Through surrender, our desires are repositioned to reflect God's character and values. Our ambitions shift from self-centered goals to desires that contribute to the betterment of ourselves and the world around us.

Scripture and prayer serve as powerful tools in the journey of transformation. Romans 12:2 (NIV) encourages us, "Do not conform to the pattern of this world, but be transformed by the renewing of your mind." By immersing ourselves in God's Word, we expose our minds to His truth, wisdom, and values, leading to the reshaping of our desires.

Prayer plays a pivotal role in this journey. Through prayer, we communicate with God, seeking His guidance, surrendering our desires, and inviting Him to transform us from the inside out. In prayer, we find the strength and wisdom needed to navigate the complexities of the heart's battleground.

The journey of transforming desires is enriched by community and accountability. Proverbs 27:17 (NIV) emphasizes this idea: "As iron sharpens iron, so one person sharpens another." Sharing our journey with trusted friends or mentors allows us to gain perspective, receive encouragement, and benefit from collective wisdom.

Accountability partners can help us stay on course, reminding us of our commitment to cultivating godly desires and holding us responsible for our choices. Through community, we find support, understanding, and a shared commitment to growth.

As we persevere on the journey of transforming desires, we discover a reward that far surpasses temporary satisfactions. Our desires become aligned with God's heart, leading us to pursue goals that are meaningful, purposeful, and eternally significant. We experience a deep sense of fulfillment that comes from living in harmony with God's will.

This transformation not only impacts our personal lives but radiates to those around us. By cultivating desires that honor God, we become beacons of His love, grace, and truth to a world in need.

The journey of transforming desires is a path toward a life transformed by God's grace. Through surrender, renewal, community, and accountability, our desires are reshaped into reflections of God's character and values. As we navigate the heart's battleground, may we embark on this journey with determination, knowing that the transformation of our desires leads us to a life of purpose, fulfillment, and lasting impact.

Chapter 4: Guarding Against Deception

"The heart is deceitful above all things and beyond cure. Who can understand it?" - Jeremiah 17:9 (NIV)

In the complex landscape of the heart's battleground, deception lurks as a cunning adversary—a force that seeks to distort truth, cloud judgment, and lead us astray from God's path. This chapter explores the critical importance of guarding against deception, recognizing its tactics, and equipping ourselves with the discernment needed to navigate the treacherous terrain.

4.1 The Nature of Deception

Deception, like a skilled illusionist, operates in the shadows of the heart's battleground, often masquerading as truth and playing on the vulnerabilities of our human nature. It's a formidable adversary that seeks to distort our perceptions, skew our judgment, and lead us down paths contrary to God's will. Understanding the nature of deception is crucial for recognizing its tactics and effectively guarding our hearts.

Deception operates by presenting distortions of reality. It takes fragments of truth, twists them, and presents a warped version of the whole picture. Just as a funhouse mirror distorts reflections, deception distorts our understanding of the world, ourselves, and even God.

Deceptive thoughts and desires often appear attractive and alluring on the surface. They promise fulfillment, pleasure, or success, masking their underlying motives. These distorted desires can lead us to chase after temporary gratifications while neglecting the deeper needs of our souls.

Deception thrives in the heart's vulnerability. Our hearts, while capable of great love and wisdom, are also susceptible to emotions, desires, and biases that can cloud our judgment. Proverbs 14:12 (NIV) warns, "There is a way that appears to be right, but in the end, it leads to death." This cautionary proverb underscores the deceitfulness of appearances and the need for discernment.

The heart's vulnerability to deception often stems from its fallen nature. As a result of sin, our hearts can be easily swayed by self-centered desires, leading us to pursue what seems right in our eyes rather than seeking God's wisdom.

The enemy, often referred to as Satan or the devil, is the mastermind behind deception. In John 8:44 (NIV), Jesus describes the devil as "the father of lies." The enemy's primary aim is to deceive and lead people away from God's truth and into spiritual darkness.

One of the enemy's tactics is to exploit our desires and weaknesses. Just as he used Eve's desire for knowledge to deceive her in the Garden of Eden, he capitalizes on our desires for success, pleasure, and significance to distort our perceptions and lead us away from God's best.

Guarding against deception requires cultivating discernment—a spiritual skill that allows us to distinguish between truth and falsehood. Discernment involves seeking God's wisdom, testing our thoughts and desires against His Word, and relying on the Holy Spirit's guidance.

Hebrews 5:14 (NIV) speaks to the importance of discernment: "But solid food is for the mature, who by constant use have trained themselves to distinguish good from evil." Just as athletes train their bodies, we must train our minds and hearts to discern the subtle nuances of truth and deception.

Recognizing the nature of deception equips us to stand vigilant against its cunning tactics. By understanding that our hearts are susceptible, we are motivated to guard our thoughts and desires with the armor of

God's truth. Through prayer, the study of Scripture, and reliance on the Holy Spirit, we navigate the heart's battleground with wisdom, ready to unmask deception and choose the path that leads to alignment with God's will.

4.2 Unmasking Deception's Tactics

Deception is a master of disguise, often cloaking itself in appealing facades that lure us away from truth and godly desires. To effectively guard against deception, we must unmask its tactics and become adept at recognizing its subtle manipulations.

Deception often presents itself as an alternative that seems attractive and beneficial. It preys on our desires for success, happiness, and significance, offering shortcuts or detours that promise immediate gratification. Just as the serpent enticed Eve with the allure of becoming "like God" by eating the forbidden fruit (Genesis 3:5), deception appeals to our desires for knowledge, power, and fulfillment.

These appealing alternatives divert our attention from God's intended path and plan for our lives. Deception tempts us to believe that we can achieve our desires without adhering to God's standards or waiting for His timing.

A hallmark of deception is its ability to distort truth by presenting half-truths. It takes a kernel of truth and wraps it in layers of misinformation, creating a misleading narrative that's difficult to unravel. Just as the serpent mixed truth ("You will not certainly die") with falsehood ("You will be like God") in deceiving Eve, deception often combines accurate information with distortions to create confusion.

This tactic capitalizes on our trust in partial truths and our tendency to fill in the gaps with assumptions. Unmasking deception requires careful examination of the information presented, seeking out the full truth rather than settling for a distorted version.

Deception thrives on doubt and fear, casting shadows of uncertainty over our thoughts and decisions. It whispers lies that undermine our confidence in God's goodness, His promises, and His plans. Just as the enemy planted doubt in the minds of Adam and Eve by questioning God's words ("Did God really say...?"), deception sows seeds of uncertainty that weaken our faith.

Doubt and fear can lead us to make hasty decisions or to second-guess the direction God is leading us. Unmasking deception involves confronting these doubts with the reassurances found in God's Word and grounding our faith in His unchanging character.

Unmasking deception requires discernment—an ability to perceive and evaluate situations, thoughts, and desires with spiritual wisdom. Hebrews 5:14 (NIV) speaks of mature believers who "have trained themselves to distinguish good from evil." Discernment involves actively seeking God's perspective, testing everything against His Word, and relying on the Holy Spirit's guidance.

By cultivating discernment, we can see through the appealing veneer of deception and identify its true nature. Discernment empowers us to recognize when a desire is motivated by self-centeredness, when a path leads away from God's will, or when an opportunity is too good to be true.

As we navigate the heart's battleground, unmasking deception's tactics is a vital skill in guarding our hearts. By understanding its methods, we become equipped to discern between truth and falsehood, between genuine desires and deceptive temptations. Through a foundation of discernment, grounded in God's Word and guided by the Holy Spirit, we develop the wisdom needed to navigate the complexities of the heart and make choices that honor God and align with His perfect will.

4.3 The Armor of Discernment

In the unrelenting battle against deception, we are not left defenseless. God equips us with a powerful armor, tailored to guard our hearts and minds against the subtle schemes of the enemy. This armor of discernment is essential for navigating the heart's battleground with wisdom, clarity, and an unwavering commitment to truth.

The first piece of the armor of discernment is the belt of truth. Just as a belt holds a warrior's armor in place, truth anchors our understanding and perception. Embracing the truth of God's Word acts as a foundation for discernment, allowing us to distinguish between falsehood and reality. Psalm 119:160 (NIV) affirms, "All your words are true; all your righteous laws are eternal."

As we immerse ourselves in Scripture and seek God's truth, we fortify our minds against the deceptions that would lead us astray. Truth exposes the distortions of deception and keeps us grounded in the unchanging character of God.

The breastplate of righteousness guards our hearts against moral compromise and impurity. This armor protects our desires from being tainted by self-centeredness and sinful motives. Philippians 4:8 (NIV) provides a guideline for this aspect of discernment: "Finally, brothers and sisters, whatever is true, whatever is noble, whatever is right, whatever is pure, whatever is lovely, whatever is admirable—if anything is excellent or praiseworthy—think about such things."

A heart covered by the breastplate of righteousness is vigilant against desires that conflict with God's standards. It seeks to cultivate godly desires that reflect His character and honor His will.

The shield of faith plays a crucial role in discernment by deflecting doubts and fears. Just as a shield protects a warrior from incoming attacks, faith shields us from the doubts and uncertainties that deception seeks to sow. Ephesians 6:16 (NIV) describes this shield: "In addition to all this, take up the shield of faith, with which you can extinguish all the flaming arrows of the evil one."

By trusting in God's promises and character, we silence the whispers of deception that seek to erode our confidence. A shield of faith allows us to move forward with discernment, knowing that God's truth is unshakable.

The helmet of salvation secures our identity in Christ and guards our minds against the lies of the enemy. When we are rooted in the assurance of our salvation, we can counteract the deceptive tactics that challenge our worth and significance. Romans 8:38-39 (NIV) assures us, "For I am convinced that neither death nor life, neither angels nor demons, neither the present nor the future, nor any powers, neither height nor depth, nor anything else in all creation, will be able to separate us from the love of God that is in Christ Jesus our Lord."

A helmet of salvation protects us from the lies that question our value and purpose, enabling us to discern desires that align with God's plan for our lives.

The final piece of the armor of discernment is the sword of the Spirit, which is the Word of God. Ephesians 6:17 (NIV) describes it as "the sword of the Spirit, which is the word of God." The Word of God serves as both an offensive and defensive weapon in the battle against deception. It allows us to confront falsehoods with the truth and to discern the motives and intentions behind desires.

By meditating on Scripture, we sharpen our ability to discern God's will and sift through the complexities of desires, motives, and decisions.

As we face the challenges of the heart's battleground, the armor of discernment becomes our steadfast protection. Through the belt of truth, the breastplate of righteousness, the shield of faith, the helmet of salvation, and the sword of the Spirit, we navigate the complexities of desires and decisions with wisdom and clarity. This armor equips us to unmask deception, choose godly desires, and stand firm in our commitment to truth, ensuring that our hearts remain guarded and aligned with God's perfect will.

4.4 The Role of Wisdom and Prayer

In the ongoing battle against deception, the interplay of wisdom and prayer becomes a dynamic force that empowers us to discern truth from falsehood, align our desires with God's will, and navigate the heart's battleground with clarity and steadfastness.

Wisdom is a treasure that allows us to see beyond the surface and perceive the deeper truths. Proverbs 4:7 (NIV) tells us, "The beginning of wisdom is this: Get wisdom. Though it cost all you have, get understanding." The pursuit of wisdom involves seeking a deep understanding of God's character, His Word, and His ways.

Wisdom is crucial in discernment because it enables us to recognize the broader implications of our desires and decisions. It helps us weigh the short-term gains against the long-term consequences, revealing the true nature of deceptive temptations.

Wisdom, in conjunction with the Word of God, forms a powerful duo for discernment. By testing our thoughts, desires, and circumstances against the truths found in Scripture, we can identify whether they align with God's character and principles. Psalm 119:105 (NIV) declares, "Your word is a lamp for my feet, a light on my path."

As we engage in the practice of Scripture meditation and study, we equip ourselves to recognize the discrepancies between deceptive desires and the godly desires that reflect God's truth.

Prayer is an essential component of guarding against deception. It is through prayer that we connect with God's wisdom, align our hearts with His will, and seek His guidance in discerning our desires. Philippians 4:6-7 (NIV) encourages us, "Do not be anxious about anything, but in every situation, by prayer and petition, with thanksgiving, present your requests to God. And the peace of God, which transcends all understanding, will guard your hearts and your minds in Christ Jesus."

In times of uncertainty and decision-making, prayer opens the door to divine insight. Through prayer, we invite God's Spirit to illuminate our minds and hearts, granting us the discernment needed to navigate the complexities of desires and guard against deception.

God often speaks to us through a still, small voice—a whisper that can easily be drowned out by the noise of worldly desires. In 1 Kings 19:11-12 (NIV), God's voice is described: "Then a great and powerful wind tore the mountains apart and shattered the rocks before the Lord, but the Lord was not in the wind. After the wind, there was an earthquake, but the Lord was not in the earthquake. After the earthquake came a fire, but the Lord was not in the fire. And after the fire came a gentle whisper."

Discernment is honed through a quiet, attentive spirit. By taking time to pray, meditate, and listen to God's still, small voice, we can discern the subtle promptings of His Spirit amidst the clamor of competing desires.

In the battle against deception, wisdom and prayer work in tandem to fortify our hearts and minds. By pursuing wisdom through Scripture, testing our desires against God's Word, and seeking God's guidance through prayer, we develop the discernment needed to distinguish between true desires and deceptive temptations.

In the stillness of prayer, we find a sanctuary where God's wisdom meets our hearts. By embracing the transformative power of wisdom and prayer, we navigate the heart's battleground with a steadfast commitment to truth and a vigilant defense against the deceptions that seek to divert us from God's perfect will.

4.5 Walking in the Light

In the midst of the heart's battleground, where deception seeks to blur the lines between truth and falsehood, walking in the light emerges as a powerful principle that illuminates our path, exposes deception's shadows, and guides us toward the truth that guards our hearts.

Walking in the light involves living in transparency and authenticity before God and others. 1 John 1:7 (NIV) states, "But if we walk in the light, as he is in the light, we have fellowship with one another, and the blood of Jesus, his Son, purifies us from all sin." Transparency dismantles the veils that deception seeks to cast over our hearts.

When we're open about our struggles, desires, and temptations, we invite accountability and support from fellow believers. This fellowship acts as a safeguard against the isolation that deception thrives in, allowing us to face our challenges with the strength of community.

Walking in the light involves approaching God with an unveiled heart. 2 Corinthians 3:18 (NIV) speaks of this transformation: "And we all, who with unveiled faces contemplate the Lord's glory, are being transformed into his image with ever-increasing glory, which comes from the Lord, who is the Spirit." As we behold God's glory, our hearts are transformed to reflect His truth.

An unveiled heart is receptive to God's Word and the leading of His Spirit. It allows us to discern the intentions behind our desires, separating godly aspirations from self-centered longings.

Walking in the light includes a willingness to confess and repent when we recognize deceptive desires or choices. 1 John 1:9 (NIV) assures us, "If we confess our sins, he is faithful and just and will forgive us our sins and purify us from all unrighteousness." Confession and repentance restore us to a place of alignment with God's truth.

Confession dismantles deception's hold by bringing our hidden desires into the light of God's grace. Repentance marks a decisive turning away from deceptive paths, enabling us to realign our desires with God's will.

Walking in the light exposes deception's darkness. Ephesians 5:11-13 (NIV) instructs, "Have nothing to do with the fruitless deeds of darkness, but rather expose them. It is shameful even to mention what the disobedient do in secret. But everything exposed by the light becomes visible."

As we live in the light of God's truth, the deceptive motives and desires that once remained hidden are brought into the open. The more we expose these hidden corners to God's truth, the more discerning we become in identifying the tactics of deception.

Walking in the light is not only a metaphorical concept but a practical lifestyle that guides our steps on the heart's battleground. By living transparently, unveiling our hearts before God, confessing and repenting, and exposing deception's darkness, we navigate the complexities of desires with God's illuminating truth.

In the light of God's presence, deception's illusions lose their power. Walking in the light empowers us to discern the motives behind our desires, make decisions that honor God's truth, and guard our hearts against the shadows of falsehood. As we choose to walk in the light, we ensure that our desires remain aligned with the brilliance of God's perfect will.

4.6 Vigilant and Grounded

To effectively guard against deception in the heart's battleground, we must adopt a posture of vigilance and remain grounded in truth. This vigilance involves staying alert to the subtle whispers of deception, while grounding ourselves in the unchanging truths of God's Word.

Vigilance demands watchful alertness to the tactics of deception that often creep into our thoughts and desires. 1 Peter 5:8 (NIV) warns, "Be alert and of sober mind. Your enemy the devil prowls around like a roaring lion looking for someone to devour." Like a watchman on a tower, we must be vigilant, scanning the horizon for any signs of deception's approach.

This alertness requires a keen awareness of our own vulnerabilities and the ways in which the enemy may exploit them. Through prayer, self-examination, and reliance on God's wisdom, we can discern the subtle shifts in our desires and motivations.

Remaining grounded in truth is our anchor against the shifting sands of deception. John 8:31-32 (NIV) highlights the connection between truth and freedom: "If you hold to my teaching, you are really my disciples. Then you will know the truth, and the truth will set you free." Embracing truth empowers us to discern the lies that deception presents.

Grounding ourselves in truth involves consistently immersing ourselves in God's Word. By meditating on Scripture, we build a strong foundation of knowledge that counteracts the misinformation deception seeks to implant in our minds.

Vigilance and grounding combine to form the lens of discernment—a perspective through which we evaluate our desires, thoughts, and decisions. Philippians 1:9-10 (NIV) speaks to this lens: "And this is my prayer: that your love may abound more and more in knowledge and depth of insight, so that you may be able to discern what is best and may be pure and blameless for the day of Christ."

Through the lens of discernment, we gain clarity on the motives behind our desires. We evaluate whether they align with God's values, whether they lead to life-giving outcomes, and whether they contribute to our growth in Christ-likeness.

Vigilance and grounding are nurtured through our continuous seeking of divine guidance. Proverbs 3:5-6 (NIV) advises, "Trust in the Lord with all your heart and lean not on your own understanding; in all your ways submit to him, and he will make your paths straight." Seeking God's guidance in prayer positions us to navigate the heart's battleground with His wisdom.

In times of decision-making, we invite God to illuminate our desires and reveal any deceptive influences. This dependence on God's guidance ensures that our choices are aligned with His perfect will.

In the heart's battleground, vigilance and grounding empower us to stand firm against deception's advances. By maintaining watchful alertness and anchoring ourselves in God's truth, we develop the lens of discernment that clarifies our desires and motives. Through seeking divine guidance, we ensure that our hearts remain guarded against the deceptive forces that seek to derail our spiritual journey.

With empowered vigilance, we engage in the ongoing battle with a steadfast commitment to truth, a discerning spirit, and an unwavering determination to honor God in every facet of our desires and decisions.

Chapter 5: The Power of Renewal

In the heart's battleground, where desires and influences collide, the power of renewal emerges as a transformative force that purifies our motives, rejuvenates our perspectives, and revitalizes our commitment to God's will. This chapter delves into the significance of embracing renewal, allowing it to shape our desires, and experiencing the profound changes it brings to our hearts and lives.

5.1 Embracing the Renewal Process

In the heart's battleground, where desires often clash and deceptive influences are ever-present, the process of renewal emerges as a beacon of hope—a divine opportunity to realign our hearts with God's purposes, cleanse our motives, and experience the transformative power of His grace.

Embracing the renewal process begins with a heart surrendered to God's transformative work. Romans 12:1 (NIV) sets the tone: "Therefore, I urge you, brothers and sisters, in view of God's mercy, to offer your bodies as a living sacrifice, holy and pleasing to God—this is your true and proper worship."

Surrender acknowledges that our desires can be tainted by self-centeredness and worldly influences. It invites God to step into the depths of our hearts, examine our motives, and lead us toward desires that are pure, noble, and in alignment with His will.

Embracing renewal also requires confronting the struggle of the flesh—the human inclination toward sinful desires. Galatians 5:17 (NIV) explains this internal conflict: "For the flesh desires what is contrary to the Spirit, and the Spirit what is contrary to the flesh. They are in conflict with each other, so that you are not to do whatever you want."

Recognizing this struggle prompts us to lean on God's grace and to seek His transformative power. The renewal process involves acknowledging our weaknesses and inviting the Holy Spirit to empower us to overcome the pull of sinful desires.

Central to the renewal process is the examination of our hearts. Psalm 139:23-24 (NIV) articulates this prayer: "Search me, God, and know my heart; test me and know my anxious thoughts. See if there is any offensive way in me, and lead me in the way everlasting."

Through introspection and prayer, we allow God's light to shine into the recesses of our hearts, exposing hidden desires, selfish motives, and areas where we have been susceptible to deception. This examination paves the way for His transformative work to cleanse and redirect our desires.

Embracing renewal requires humility and a teachable spirit. James 4:6 (NIV) reminds us, "But he gives us more grace. That is why Scripture says: 'God opposes the proud but shows favor to the humble.'" A humble heart acknowledges our need for God's guidance and recognizes that our desires can be clouded by pride.

Being teachable means that we are open to correction and willing to shift our desires to align with God's truth. It involves a willingness to change, to let go of desires that do not honor God, and to embrace desires that are rooted in His purposes.

Embracing the renewal process is an acknowledgment of our ongoing need for God's work in our lives. It is a journey that involves surrender, wrestling with the flesh, examining our hearts, and embracing humility. As we invite God to renew our desires, we embark on a transformative journey where He purifies our motives, redirects our aspirations, and guides us toward desires that are consistent with His perfect will.

Through this process, we experience a profound transformation—a transformation that affects not only our desires but also our thoughts, actions, and character. As we yield to the power of renewal, we become vessels through which God's transformative grace shines, illuminating the battleground of the heart with His radiant truth.

5.2 Cleansing and Purification

In the heart's battleground, where desires often wrestle with the allure of deception, the process of renewal takes on the role of a spiritual cleansing—a purifying journey that washes away impurities, redirects motives, and readies the heart for a closer walk with God.

Cleansing is at the heart of renewal, for our desires are susceptible to the stains of self-centeredness, worldly influences, and sinful tendencies. Psalm 51:10 (NIV) expresses the plea for cleansing: "Create in me a pure heart, O God, and renew a steadfast spirit within me." This cry acknowledges the impurities that can taint our desires and seeks the purifying touch of God.

Just as metals are refined through fire to remove impurities, so the renewal process involves the fire of God's refining grace, which purges our hearts of desires that are not in harmony with His holiness.

As renewal takes place, a shift occurs in our desires. What once drew us towards selfish gain or worldly ambitions now begins to draw us closer to God's heart. This transformation aligns our desires with His perfect will, as our motives are purified by the refining fire of His love.

Galatians 5:22-23 (NIV) beautifully outlines the fruits of the Spirit: "But the fruit of the Spirit is love, joy, peace, forbearance, kindness, goodness, faithfulness, gentleness and self-control." These qualities reflect the transformative work of renewal in cleansing our desires and bearing the fruit of godly aspirations.

Cleansing and purification through renewal result in a heart transformed by God's grace. Ezekiel 36:26-27 (NIV) captures this promise: "I will give you a new heart and put a new spirit in you; I will remove from you your heart of stone and give you a heart of flesh. And I will put my Spirit in you and move you to follow my decrees and be careful to keep my laws."

A heart transformed by renewal is marked by a deep desire to live in alignment with God's will. This transformed heart no longer pursues self-serving desires but seeks after what pleases God and furthers His kingdom.

Cleansing and purification drive us towards a life of holiness. 2 Corinthians 7:1 (NIV) exhorts, "Therefore, since we have these promises, dear friends, let us purify ourselves from everything that contaminates body and spirit, perfecting holiness out of reverence for God."

Holiness is the natural outcome of a heart cleansed and renewed. It is a commitment to pursue desires that are set apart for God's purposes, seeking to honor Him in all aspects of life.

The cleansing and purification brought about by renewal is a testament to God's redemptive power. As we surrender our desires to His refining fire, we emerge with hearts that are cleansed, motives that are purified, and desires that are aligned with His truth.

Renewal not only washes away impurities but also unveils the beauty of desires that are transformed by God's grace. These desires reflect the character of Christ and resonate with eternal significance. In the heart's battleground, the power of cleansing through renewal shines as a beacon of hope—a process that not only renews our desires but transforms our entire being into vessels that radiate God's love and light.

5.3 Shifting Perspectives

In the heart's battleground, where desires and influences compete for our attention, the process of renewal brings about a profound shifting of perspectives—a transformative change in how we view our desires, priorities, and the world around us. This shift empowers us to see through the lens of God's truth and align our aspirations with His eternal purposes.

Renewal invites us to see through God's lens—to view the world, our desires, and our decisions from His perspective. Isaiah 55:8-9 (NIV) reminds us, "For my thoughts are not your thoughts, neither are your ways my ways... As the heavens are higher than the earth, so are my ways higher than your ways and my thoughts than your thoughts."

Shifting our perspective involves acknowledging that our human understanding is limited and seeking the wisdom that comes from aligning our thoughts with God's truth. As we do so, our desires begin to align with His perfect plan.

Renewal prompts us to shift our focus from the temporary to the eternal. Colossians 3:2 (NIV) advises, "Set your minds on things above, not on earthly things." This shift in perspective reminds us that earthly desires and achievements, while valuable, must be viewed in the context of eternity.

As our desires are renewed, we begin to prioritize the pursuits that have lasting significance—building God's kingdom, investing in relationships, and seeking righteousness. This shift leads to a more purposeful and fulfilling life.

Shifting perspectives through renewal allows us to glimpse God's purposes in our desires and circumstances. Romans 8:28 (NIV) reassures us, "And we know that in all things God works for the good of those who love him, who have been called according to his purpose."

In the midst of challenges and desires that seem conflicting, a renewed perspective enables us to see how God is working all things together for His ultimate purposes. This understanding grants us the assurance that our desires, when aligned with His will, contribute to His greater plan.

Renewed perspectives often lead to a heart of gratitude. Ephesians 5:20 (NIV) encourages, "always giving thanks to God the Father for everything, in the name of our Lord Jesus Christ." When we shift our focus from what we lack to the blessings we have, our desires are infused with a spirit of contentment and gratitude.

A heart of gratitude transforms the way we view our desires—less as insatiable needs and more as opportunities to celebrate God's goodness.

Shifting perspectives through renewal is a transformative journey that changes the way we approach desires, decisions, and life itself. As we see through God's lens, prioritize the eternal, glimpse His purposes, and cultivate a heart of gratitude, our desires undergo a profound transformation.

Renewed perspectives lead to desires that are aligned with God's truth and characterized by a sense of purpose, contentment, and joy. In the heart's battleground, where conflicting desires vie for attention, the power of shifted perspectives illuminates the path to a life that radiates the brilliance of God's eternal purposes.

5.4 The Role of Surrender

In the heart's battleground, where desires often clash and deceptive influences persist, surrender emerges as a pivotal force in the process of renewal. Surrender involves yielding our desires, motives, and will to God's transformative work—a transformative work that purifies our aspirations and leads us to desires aligned with His perfect will.

Surrender is an act of laying down our desires before the throne of God. It is an acknowledgment that our own understanding and inclinations can be flawed, and an invitation for God to reshape them according to His wisdom. Proverbs 3:5-6 (NIV) advises, "Trust in the Lord with all your heart and lean not on your own understanding; in all your ways submit to him, and he will make your paths straight."

A surrendered heart recognizes that God's plans and desires for us are higher and better than our own. It acknowledges that our desires must be filtered through the lens of His truth and subjected to His guidance.

Surrender involves letting go of the need for control and trusting in God's sovereignty. Psalm 37:5 (NIV) encourages, "Commit your way to the Lord; trust in him and he will do this." When we surrender, we release our grip on the outcomes and entrust our desires to the One who knows what is best for us.

Letting go of control may feel daunting, but it is liberating. It frees us from the burden of making decisions solely based on our limited perspective and empowers us to make choices that align with God's greater plan.

Surrender also means renouncing self-centeredness and embracing a Christ-centered focus. Galatians 2:20 (NIV) captures this essence: "I have been crucified with Christ and I no longer live, but Christ lives in me." Surrender involves crucifying our selfish desires and inviting Christ to dwell within us.

As we surrender, our desires shift from seeking personal gratification to seeking God's glory and the well-being of others. Selfish ambitions are replaced with desires that reflect the character of Christ.

Often, hidden desires reside deep within our hearts, influencing our thoughts and decisions. Surrender involves bringing these hidden desires into the light of God's truth. Psalm 139:23-24 (NIV) captures this prayer, "Search me, God, and know my heart; test me and know my anxious thoughts. See if there is any offensive way in me, and lead me in the way everlasting."

Releasing hidden desires through surrender allows God to expose them, purify them, and guide us toward desires that are in harmony with His nature.

Surrender is a continuous process—a daily yielding of our desires and will to God's transforming grace. As we surrender, our desires are purified, our motives are refined, and our hearts are shaped into vessels that honor God.

A life of surrender is not a life of resignation but of empowerment. It empowers us to live in alignment with God's will, make decisions that honor Him, and pursue desires that reflect His love and truth. In the heart's battleground, where desires contend for dominance, surrender becomes a beacon of hope—a choice that leads us to desires that are infused with the power of God's transformative work.

5.5 Experiencing Lasting Change

Amidst the heart's battleground, where desires and influences collide, the process of renewal brings about a profound and lasting change—a transformation that goes beyond surface adjustments and penetrates deep into the core of our being. This transformation not only impacts our desires but also reshapes our thoughts, actions, and the trajectory of our lives.

Experiencing lasting change through renewal ushers in a sense of becoming a new creation. 2 Corinthians 5:17 (NIV) declares, "Therefore, if anyone is in Christ, the new creation has come: The old has gone, the new is here!" This transformation is marked by a renewal of desires, a reorientation of priorities, and a redirection of our hearts towards God's purposes.

As our desires are renewed, we find ourselves drawn towards pursuits that align with God's will and contribute to the advancement of His kingdom.

Lasting change through renewal is marked by consistency—a steadfast commitment to living out the transformed desires that have emerged from the renewal process. Romans 12:2 (NIV) exhorts us, "Do not conform to the pattern of this world, but be transformed by the renewing of your mind. Then you will be able to test and approve what God's will is—his good, pleasing and perfect will."

Consistency involves making daily choices that reflect our renewed desires and align with the truth of God's Word. It means resisting the pull of old, self-centered desires and instead embracing desires that reflect the character of Christ.

Experiencing lasting change through renewal results in a transformed lifestyle. This transformation affects the way we relate to others, the decisions we make, and the choices we prioritize. Galatians 5:22-23 (NIV) beautifully captures the essence of this transformation: "But the fruit of the Spirit is love, joy, peace, forbearance, kindness, goodness, faithfulness, gentleness and self-control."

A transformed lifestyle is characterized by the fruit of the Spirit—qualities that emanate from a heart that has been renewed and purified.

Lasting change through renewal leads us to walk in obedience to God's commands. 1 John 5:3 (NIV) reminds us, "In fact, this is love for God: to keep his commands. And his commands are not burdensome." As our desires are renewed, we find joy in aligning our choices with His will.

Walking in obedience is a natural outflow of a heart that has been transformed. Our renewed desires lead us to willingly follow God's leading and seek His guidance in every aspect of life.

Experiencing lasting change through renewal is a testament to the power of God's transformative grace. As our desires are purified, redirected, and aligned with His truth, we embark on a journey of transformation that encompasses our entire being.

The changes we experience through renewal go beyond the temporary—they are lasting and enduring. They shape our character, influence our relationships, and guide our decisions. In the heart's battleground, where desires contend for supremacy, the power of lasting change through renewal shines as a beacon of hope—a process that not only transforms our desires but also leaves an indelible mark on our lives, reflecting the beauty of a heart that has been renewed by the Creator's loving hands.

5.6 Transformed Desires, Transformed Life

In the heart's battleground, where desires often clash and deceptive influences persist, the transformative power of renewal extends beyond isolated changes to encompass every facet of our existence. Transformed desires, resulting from the renewal process, pave the way for a wholly transformed life—one marked by alignment with God's truth, pursuit of His purposes, and a reflection of His character.

Transformed desires serve as evidence of an internal transformation—a renewal of the heart that ripples outward to influence our thoughts, emotions, and decisions. Ezekiel 36:26 (NIV) encapsulates this transformation: "I will give you a new heart and put a new spirit in you; I will remove from you your heart of stone and give you a heart of flesh."

As our desires are renewed, we experience a shift from self-centeredness to God-centeredness, from worldly pursuits to eternal significance.

This internal transformation shapes the way we view ourselves, others, and the world around us.

Transformed desires guide us towards a life of purpose—a life infused with God's calling and His kingdom's priorities. Psalm 37:4 (NIV) encourages us, "Take delight in the Lord, and he will give you the desires of your heart." This promise underscores the connection between delighting in God and having desires aligned with His will.

As we delight in God, our desires are molded by His desires. The transformed desires that emerge from the renewal process lead us to pursue God's purposes and contribute to His redemptive work in the world.

Transformed desires result in a life that reflects the character of Christ. Galatians 5:22-23 (NIV) beautifully outlines the fruit of the Spirit: "But the fruit of the Spirit is love, joy, peace, forbearance, kindness, goodness, faithfulness, gentleness and self-control."

As our desires are renewed, we are empowered to manifest these qualities in our interactions and relationships. Our transformed desires lead us to love as Christ loves, to show kindness and grace, and to exercise self-control in our actions and decisions.

Transformed desires empower us to overcome the challenges of the heart's battleground. 1 John 5:4 (NIV) assures us, "for everyone born of God overcomes the world. This is the victory that has overcome the world, even our faith."

The victory over the conflicting desires, temptations, and influences of the world is fueled by the transformed desires that arise from the renewal process. These desires are grounded in faith, supported by the power of the Holy Spirit, and fueled by a passion to honor God.

Transformed desires, resulting from the renewal process, usher in a transformed life—a life marked by purpose, character, and victory. The legacy of this transformation extends beyond our individual journeys to impact those around us.

As we navigate the heart's battleground with desires that are renewed and aligned with God's will, we become beacons of hope and inspiration for others who seek the transformative power of renewal. Our transformed lives serve as testimonies to the grace and work of God, inviting others to experience the same life-changing renewal that has shaped our desires and guided our steps.

In the journey from transformed desires to transformed life, we find ourselves immersed in the wondrous journey of being continually molded into the image of Christ, whose desires are perfect and whose life is our ultimate example.

Chapter 6: Filling the Heart with Goodness

In the heart's battleground, where desires and influences vie for dominance, the call to fill our hearts with goodness emerges as a powerful antidote to the pull of deception and self-centered desires. This chapter explores the significance of cultivating a heart that is saturated with goodness, seeking to understand its impact on desires, decisions, and relationships.

6.1 The Pursuit of Goodness

In the heart's battleground, where desires and influences often collide, the pursuit of goodness emerges as a transformative journey—a deliberate endeavor to align our hearts with the character of God and to infuse our desires with His pure and righteous nature.

The pursuit of goodness is, at its core, a quest to reflect the character of God. Psalm 145:9 (NIV) beautifully captures this truth: "The Lord is good to all; he has compassion on all he has made." As we seek goodness, we aim to emulate the heart of our Creator, who is the source of all goodness.

Choosing goodness is an acknowledgment of God's nature as the ultimate standard of what is right, just, and pure. It involves cultivating desires that mirror His heart of compassion, kindness, and love.

The pursuit of goodness is a response to God's call for us to walk in His ways. Micah 6:8 (NIV) encapsulates this call: "He has shown you, O mortal, what is good. And what does the Lord require of you? To act justly and to love mercy and to walk humbly with your God."

Responding to this call means aligning our desires with justice, mercy, and humility. It means actively seeking to cultivate desires that are pleasing to God and that contribute to the well-being of others.

In a world that often promotes self-centered desires, the pursuit of goodness serves as a counterbalance. Romans 12:21 (NIV) urges us, "Do not be overcome by evil, but overcome evil with good." The pursuit of goodness involves resisting the pull of selfish desires and choosing instead to be agents of positive change.

By pursuing goodness, we allow our desires to be shaped by values that transcend personal gain and seek the welfare of others. This counters the corrosive influence of self-centeredness.

The pursuit of goodness involves cultivating virtuous desires that honor God and reflect His kingdom values. Philippians 4:8 (NIV) provides a blueprint for such cultivation: "Finally, brothers and sisters, whatever is true, whatever is noble, whatever is right, whatever is pure, whatever is lovely, whatever is admirable—if anything is excellent or praiseworthy—think about such things."

As we fill our minds with virtuous thoughts, our desires undergo a transformation. The pursuit of goodness leads to desires that are centered on truth, purity, and excellence.

The pursuit of goodness is not a mere ideal but a transformative journey that molds our desires, decisions, and character. It requires intentionality, humility, and a commitment to align our hearts with the heart of God.

In the heart's battleground, where conflicting desires often wage war, the pursuit of goodness stands as a beacon of light—a choice that draws us closer to God's nature and empowers us to infuse our desires with His pure and righteous attributes. As we journey in the pursuit of goodness, we find ourselves becoming vessels through which God's goodness flows, radiating His light in a world hungry for the transformative power of virtuous desires.

6.2 The Transformation of Desires

Amidst the heart's battleground, where desires can lead astray and deceptive influences persist, the pursuit of goodness leads to a profound transformation of desires—a renewal that redirects our longings and shapes them in accordance with God's perfect will.

The pursuit of goodness triggers a shift in the focus of our desires. Instead of being fixated on fleeting pleasures or self-centered gain, our desires become centered on what is pure, noble, and pleasing to God. Romans 12:2 (NIV) encapsulates this transformation: "Do not conform to the pattern of this world, but be transformed by the renewing of your mind."

As our minds are renewed through the pursuit of goodness, our desires begin to align with God's desires, leading us to seek His kingdom and righteousness above all else.

The pursuit of goodness shapes our desires to be aligned with truth and righteousness. Psalm 119:37 (NIV) expresses this desire: "Turn my eyes away from worthless things; preserve my life according to your word." Through the pursuit of goodness, we seek desires that are grounded in the unchanging truth of God's Word.

Desires transformed by goodness become desires that honor God's commandments, reflect His wisdom, and contribute to a life that is pleasing in His sight.

The transformation of desires through the pursuit of goodness redirects our yearnings toward the eternal. Colossians 3:1-2 (NIV) guides this redirection: "Since, then, you have been raised with Christ, set your hearts on things above, where Christ is, seated at the right hand of God. Set your minds on things above, not on earthly things."

In choosing goodness, we set our hearts on desires that have lasting significance. The pursuit of goodness prompts us to value heavenly treasures over temporary pleasures.

The transformation of desires through the pursuit of goodness is an expression of love—love for God and love for others. 1 Corinthians 14:1 (NIV) encourages this expression: "Follow the way of love and eagerly desire gifts of the Spirit."

As we pursue goodness, our desires become vehicles for love. We desire to serve, bless, and uplift others, aligning our desires with Christ's example of selfless love.

The transformation of desires through the pursuit of goodness is a remarkable journey of aligning our hearts with God's heart. It involves a deliberate choice to shift our focus, realign our desires with truth, embrace eternal values, and manifest love in all that we yearn for.

In the heart's battleground, where conflicting desires often pull us in different directions, the transformation of desires stands as a testament to the power of pursuing goodness. As our desires are renewed and transformed, we find ourselves drawn closer to God's perfect will, reflecting the brilliance of a heart that is being continually shaped by His goodness and grace.

6.3 A Filter for Decision-Making

In the heart's battleground, where desires and influences compete for our attention, the pursuit of goodness equips us with a powerful filter for decision-making—a lens through which we can assess our desires, discern their alignment with God's will, and make choices that honor His character.

The pursuit of goodness provides us with a clear standard for discerning the alignment of our desires with God's will. Proverbs 2:7 (NIV) speaks of God's role in decision-making: "He holds success in store for the upright, he is a shield to those whose walk is blameless."

When we seek goodness, our desires are shaped by values such as justice, mercy, and humility. This shaping enables us to assess our desires and determine whether they reflect God's heart and align with His truth.

The pursuit of goodness empowers us to choose wisdom over impulse in our decision-making. James 3:17 (NIV) describes the wisdom that arises from goodness: "But the wisdom that comes from heaven is first of all pure; then peace-loving, considerate, submissive, full of mercy and good fruit, impartial and sincere."

When we filter our desires through the lens of goodness, we make decisions that are characterized by prudence, compassion, and consideration for others. Goodness acts as a counterbalance to rash decisions driven by selfish desires.

A filter of goodness prioritizes God's glory in decision-making. 1 Corinthians 10:31 (NIV) directs us: "So whether you eat or drink or whatever you do, do it all for the glory of God." The pursuit of goodness urges us to consider whether our desires and decisions ultimately bring glory to God.

By evaluating our desires against the backdrop of goodness, we ensure that our choices are marked by a desire to honor God rather than satisfy self-centered desires.

A filter of goodness enables us to approach decision-making with compassion and empathy. Colossians 3:12 (NIV) encourages us: "Therefore, as God's chosen people, holy and dearly loved, clothe yourselves with compassion, kindness, humility, gentleness and patience."

When our desires are filtered through goodness, we are prompted to make decisions that reflect these qualities. We become more attuned to the impact of our choices on others and strive to act in ways that uplift and benefit those around us.

The pursuit of goodness provides us with a guiding light in decision-making—a filter that helps us navigate the complexities of the heart's battleground. As we intentionally seek to align our desires with God's goodness, we gain a discerning perspective that shapes our decisions according to His will.

In a world where deceptive influences can distort our desires, the filter of goodness acts as a safeguard—a tool that ensures our choices are rooted in values that honor God and reflect His character. As we filter our desires through goodness, we find ourselves making decisions that bear the mark of Christ's love, wisdom, and righteousness—a testament to the transformative power of pursuing a heart filled with goodness.

6.4 Cultivating Healthy Relationships

In the heart's battleground, where desires and influences collide, the pursuit of goodness holds the key to cultivating and nurturing healthy relationships. Goodness becomes a foundation upon which our interactions are built, fostering connections that are marked by respect, compassion, and mutual edification.

Cultivating healthy relationships through the pursuit of goodness begins with an expression of respect for others. Philippians 2:3-4 (NIV) captures this essence: "Do nothing out of selfish ambition or vain conceit. Rather, in humility value others above yourselves, not looking to your own interests but each of you to the interests of the others."

As we seek goodness, our desires are transformed into a genuine desire to honor and value those around us. This respect becomes a cornerstone for building relationships that are characterized by dignity and empathy.

Goodness paves the way for fostering compassion in relationships. Ephesians 4:32 (NIV) encourages us to "be kind and compassionate to one another, forgiving each other, just as in Christ God forgave you." The pursuit of goodness compels us to cultivate desires that mirror Christ's compassion for others.

In cultivating compassion, our desires are directed toward understanding, supporting, and showing empathy for those we interact with. It prompts us to prioritize the well-being of others and extends grace in times of conflict or misunderstanding.

Cultivating healthy relationships through goodness involves a commitment to edify and uplift others. 1 Thessalonians 5:11 (NIV) urges us: "Therefore encourage one another and build each other up, just as in fact you are doing."

The pursuit of goodness shapes our desires into a yearning to encourage, affirm, and uplift those we encounter. Our interactions become a source of strength and positivity, fostering an environment of mutual growth and support.

Goodness plays a crucial role in extending forgiveness within relationships. Colossians 3:13 (NIV) reminds us to "bear with each other and forgive one another if any of you has a grievance against someone. Forgive as the Lord forgave you."

Through the pursuit of goodness, our desires are directed toward forgiveness and reconciliation. We are motivated to let go of grudges, to seek resolution, and to prioritize the restoration of relationships over personal grievances.

The pursuit of goodness holds the transformative power to reshape our interactions and relationships. By intentionally cultivating desires that reflect God's goodness, we create an atmosphere of respect, compassion, edification, and forgiveness.

In the heart's battleground, where misunderstandings and conflicts can erode relationships, the cultivation of healthy connections through goodness becomes a beacon of hope—a way to transcend selfish desires and build connections that mirror the love and grace of Christ. As our desires are guided by goodness, our relationships become a testament to the transformation that occurs when hearts are filled with the pure and selfless desires that flow from the pursuit of God's goodness.

6.5 The Overflow of Love

In the heart's battleground, where desires and influences vie for supremacy, the pursuit of goodness leads to a beautiful overflow of love—a love that emanates from the depths of a heart transformed by the goodness of God. This overflow of love becomes a transformative force that impacts not only our desires but also our interactions, attitudes, and the way we engage with the world.

The overflow of love through the pursuit of goodness is a reflection of God's love for us. 1 John 4:7-8 (NIV) encapsulates this truth: "Dear friends, let us love one another, for love comes from God. Everyone who loves has been born of God and knows God. Whoever does not love does not know God, because God is love."

As we seek goodness, our desires are refined to mirror God's unconditional love. This overflow of love becomes a testimony to our connection with God, as it mirrors His very nature.

The overflow of love through the pursuit of goodness translates into love in action. Romans 12:9-10 (NIV) guides us: "Love must be sincere. Hate what is evil; cling to what is good. Be devoted to one another in love. Honor one another above yourselves."

Through the pursuit of goodness, our desires are directed toward practical expressions of love—acts of kindness, selflessness, and sacrifice that demonstrate our commitment to the well-being of others.

The overflow of love serves as a magnet for positive and enriching relationships. 1 Corinthians 13:4-7 (NIV) provides a poignant description of love: "Love is patient, love is kind. It does not envy, it does not boast, it is not proud. It does not dishonor others, it is not self-seeking, it is not easily angered, it keeps no record of wrongs. Love does not delight in evil but rejoices with the truth. It always protects, always trusts, always hopes, always perseveres."

When our desires overflow with love, we naturally gravitate toward relationships that embody these qualities. This overflow of love fosters connections marked by trust, mutual support, and the celebration of each other's successes.

The overflow of love through the pursuit of goodness extends beyond personal relationships to impact the world around us. John 13:35 (NIV) highlights this impact: "By this everyone will know that you are my disciples, if you love one another."

As our desires overflow with love, they become a powerful testimony of Christ's presence within us. This overflow of love becomes a source of light in a world that often craves genuine, selfless expressions of care and compassion.

The overflow of love through the pursuit of goodness is a testament to the transformative power of God's grace. As our desires are shaped by His goodness, they become channels through which His love flows—impacting our relationships, interactions, and the world at large.

In the heart's battleground, where desires can be tainted by self-interest, the overflow of love stands as a beacon of hope—a reminder of the boundless capacity of a heart that is continually filled with God's goodness. This overflow of love becomes a legacy of a life transformed, radiating the transformative and selfless nature of Christ's love to a world that is hungry for such profound expressions of care and compassion.

6.6 A Heart Transformed by Goodness

In the heart's battleground, where desires and influences wage war, the pursuit of goodness becomes a transformative journey—a journey that shapes a heart in profound ways, leading to a character marked by integrity, love, and a deep alignment with God's purposes.

The pursuit of goodness results in an inner renewal—a transformation that goes beyond surface changes and penetrates to the core of our being. Romans 12:2 (NIV) reminds us, "Do not conform to the pattern of this world, but be transformed by the renewing of your mind."

As we pursue goodness, our desires undergo a radical shift. The renewal of our desires leads to thoughts, attitudes, and actions that reflect God's character and His heart of compassion.

The pursuit of goodness molds our character into one of integrity and authenticity. Psalm 25:21 (NIV) expresses this desire: "May integrity and uprightness protect me, because my hope, Lord, is in you."

Goodness shapes desires that prioritize honesty, humility, and moral uprightness. As our desires are transformed, our character becomes a testament to the transformational power of pursuing God's goodness.

The pursuit of goodness sets our hearts on the values of God's kingdom. Matthew 6:33 (NIV) guides this alignment: "But seek first his kingdom and his righteousness, and all these things will be given to you as well."

Through the pursuit of goodness, our desires are redirected toward seeking God's purposes above all else. This transformation aligns our hearts with His will and ignites a passion to contribute to the advancement of His kingdom.

A heart transformed by goodness bears the fruit of the Spirit. Galatians 5:22-23 (NIV) highlights this transformation: "But the fruit of the Spirit is love, joy, peace, forbearance, kindness, goodness, faithfulness, gentleness and self-control."

As we pursue goodness, our desires lead to actions that naturally manifest these qualities. This transformation is a testament to the depth of change that occurs when our desires are aligned with God's goodness.

The pursuit of goodness is a journey that leads to a heart transformed by God's grace. This transformation shapes our character, desires, and actions in ways that reflect His goodness to the world.

In the heart's battleground, where conflicting desires often pull us away from God's will, a heart transformed by goodness stands as a beacon of hope—a constant reminder of the power of pursuing desires that mirror the heart of our Creator.

As our desires are continually molded by God's goodness, our transformed heart becomes a testimony to His transformative work, shining as a light in a world that is longing for the beauty, truth, and selflessness that come from a heart wholly aligned with His goodness.

Chapter 7: Community and Accountability

In the heart's battleground, where desires and influences intertwine, the role of community and accountability emerges as a crucial factor in our pursuit of goodness and the transformation of our desires. This chapter explores the significance of surrounding ourselves with a supportive community and embracing accountability to foster growth, discernment, and a heart that reflects God's goodness.

7.1 The Power of Community

In the heart's battleground, where desires and influences wrestle for dominance, the power of community emerges as a foundational force that can shape our pursuit of goodness and the transformation of our desires. Together, we explore the profound impact that surrounding ourselves with a supportive community holds in our journey of faith and growth.

Community offers strength in unity. Ecclesiastes 4:9-10 (NIV) aptly illustrates this truth: "Two are better than one, because they have a good return for their labor: If either of them falls down, one can help the other up."

In a community that shares a common pursuit of goodness, our desires are not solitary endeavors but joint efforts. The collective support and encouragement uplift us when we stumble, offering a helping hand that bolsters our resolve to align our desires with God's goodness.

Community thrives on shared experiences. Acts 2:42-47 (NIV) portrays the early Christian community's shared life: "They devoted themselves to the apostles' teaching and to fellowship, to the breaking of bread and to prayer."

In a community, our desires are influenced by the experiences and testimonies of others. These shared stories of growth, challenges, and triumphs provide guidance and inspiration, serving as a wellspring of wisdom for navigating the complexities of the heart's battleground.

Community offers mutual encouragement. Hebrews 10:24-25 (NIV) urges believers to "spur one another on toward love and good deeds, not giving up meeting together, as some are in the habit of doing, but encouraging one another."

Within a supportive community, our desires find strength through encouragement. As we share our aspirations and challenges, we inspire one another to persevere in the pursuit of goodness. This encouragement becomes a catalyst that propels us forward on our journey of transformation.

Community provides a balance of accountability and compassion. Galatians 6:1-2 (NIV) speaks to this balance: "Brothers and sisters, if someone is caught in a sin, you who live by the Spirit should restore that person gently. But watch yourselves, or you also may be tempted. Carry each other's burdens, and in this way you will fulfill the law of Christ."

Through accountability, our desires are held to a standard of goodness. Yet, this accountability is rooted in a spirit of compassion and restoration, ensuring that our pursuit of goodness is marked by both truth and grace.

The power of community in the heart's battleground is undeniable. As we surround ourselves with a community of believers who share our desire for transformation, we create a space where our desires are nurtured, encouraged, and refined.

In a world where the distractions and conflicts of desires can lead us astray, the power of community stands as a beacon of hope—a constant reminder that we are not alone in our pursuit of God's goodness. Together, we journey toward desires that reflect His character and purposes, finding strength, guidance, and inspiration in the collective pursuit of aligning our hearts with His will. Through the bonds of community, we discover the transformative and sustaining power of unity in our quest for a heart that radiates the goodness of our Creator.

7.2 Iron Sharpening Iron

Amidst the heart's battleground, where desires and influences clash, the concept of "iron sharpening iron" stands as a potent metaphor for the role of accountability within a supportive community. This powerful imagery from Proverbs 27:17 (NIV) encapsulates the transformative nature of mutual accountability as we pursue goodness and seek to transform our desires.

"Iron sharpening iron" speaks to the idea that just as one piece of iron sharpens another, individuals within a community have the capacity to refine and improve one another. In the context of pursuing goodness, our desires are the iron that is sharpened through the process of accountability.

Within a community, our desires are exposed to the insight, perspective, and wisdom of others. Through candid conversations, shared experiences, and intentional discussions, our desires are refined, honed, and aligned with God's goodness.

Accountability helps us identify blind spots that might otherwise go unnoticed. James 5:16 (NIV) encourages us: "Therefore confess your sins to each other and pray for each other so that you may be healed. The prayer of a righteous person is powerful and effective."

In a community that values accountability, our desires are subjected to the scrutiny of trusted individuals who are genuinely invested in our growth. They help us recognize areas where our desires might be influenced by deceit or self-centeredness, offering a mirror that reflects the truth of our hearts.

Accountability aids in realigning our desires with truth and righteousness. Galatians 6:1-2 (NIV) illustrates this concept: "Brothers and sisters, if someone is caught in a sin, you who live by the Spirit should restore that person gently. But watch yourselves, or you also may be tempted. Carry each other's burdens, and in this way you will fulfill the law of Christ."

Through accountability, our desires are directed toward God's standards of goodness. Trusted accountability partners help us navigate the complexities of the heart's battleground by encouraging us to prioritize desires that honor God and serve others.

Accountability fosters trust and vulnerability within a community. Ephesians 4:15 (NIV) emphasizes the importance of speaking the truth in love: "Instead, speaking the truth in love, we will grow to become in every respect the mature body of him who is the head, that is, Christ."

In a community of accountability, our desires are shared openly, and we are willing to receive both encouragement and constructive criticism. This vulnerability builds trust, allowing us to offer and receive guidance in a spirit of genuine care.

"Iron sharpening iron" underscores the transformation that occurs when we submit our desires to the process of mutual accountability within a community. As we engage in authentic conversations, share our struggles, and allow others to speak into our lives, our desires are refined and aligned with God's goodness.

In the heart's battleground, where our desires can be influenced by deception, selfishness, and worldly values, the concept of accountability stands as a safeguard—a reminder that we are not alone in our pursuit of God's best for our lives. Through the refining fires of accountability, our desires are honed into instruments that reflect the transformative power of God's truth and love, ultimately shaping us into individuals whose hearts are increasingly aligned with His perfect will.

7.3 Shared Growth and Encouragement

Within the heart's battleground, where desires and influences wage war, the power of shared growth and encouragement within a community becomes evident. This section explores how the bonds of community and the practice of mutual encouragement shape our pursuit of goodness and transformation of desires.

Shared growth is a hallmark of a supportive community. Acts 2:42-47 (NIV) paints a vivid picture of the early Christian community's shared life: "They devoted themselves to the apostles' teaching and to fellowship, to the breaking of bread and to prayer."

In a community, our desires are nurtured within an environment of mutual support and shared aspirations. This collective journey of growth inspires us to pursue goodness more intentionally as we witness the transformative power of God's work in the lives of those around us.

Mutual encouragement is a lifeline during challenges. Hebrews 10:24-25 (NIV) encourages believers to "spur one another on toward love and good deeds, not giving up meeting together, as some are in the habit of doing, but encouraging one another—and all the more as you see the Day approaching."

In a community that values mutual encouragement, our desires find strength in the midst of trials. The support of others becomes a source of motivation, reminding us that we are not alone in our pursuit of goodness.

Shared testimonies inspire growth and transformation. Revelation 12:11 (NIV) speaks of the power of testimony: "They triumphed over him by the blood of the Lamb and by the word of their testimony."

Within a community, our desires are shaped by the stories of transformation and triumph shared by others. These testimonies remind us of God's faithfulness and provide evidence that our pursuit of goodness is not in vain.

Community offers a space to uplift one another's burdens. Galatians 6:2 (NIV) emphasizes this concept: "Carry each other's burdens, and in this way you will fulfill the law of Christ."

In a community that practices mutual encouragement, our desires are oriented toward caring for one another. We become conduits of God's love by offering help, prayer, and support to those whose desires are weighed down by challenges.

Shared growth and encouragement are pivotal in nurturing the transformation of our desires within the heart's battleground. In a world where self-centered desires and external influences can erode our pursuit of goodness, the bonds of community and the practice of mutual encouragement stand as pillars of strength.

Through the shared journey of growth, the inspiration of shared testimonies, and the uplifting of one another's burdens, our desires are nurtured and refined. Within a community that values shared growth and encouragement, we find a fertile ground where our pursuit of goodness is enriched by the collective wisdom, support, and testimonies of fellow believers. As we journey together toward desires that reflect God's character, we discover the transformative power of unity and mutual encouragement in our quest for a heart that resonates with His perfect will.

7.4 Guarding Against Deception

Within the heart's battleground, where desires and influences can lead us astray, the role of community and accountability in guarding against deception becomes paramount. This section delves into the crucial aspect of how being part of a supportive community aids in discerning deceptive influences and maintaining alignment with God's goodness.

Accountability serves as a safeguard against deception. 1 Thessalonians 5:21-22 (NIV) directs believers: "Test everything; hold on to what is good, reject every kind of evil."

In a community of accountability, our desires are held to the scrutiny of trusted companions who share the common goal of pursuing goodness. These partners help us recognize when our desires are being influenced by deceitful ideas or self-serving motives.

Collective wisdom aids in discernment. Proverbs 11:14 (NIV) emphasizes the value of guidance: "For lack of guidance a nation falls, but victory is won through many advisers."

In a community that values discernment, our desires benefit from the insights and perspectives of others. As we engage in candid conversations and seek advice from trusted mentors, our desires are exposed to diverse viewpoints that aid us in making informed decisions.

Community fosters unity in pursuit of truth. Ephesians 4:14-15 (NIV) speaks to the importance of unity and growth: "Then we will no longer be infants, tossed back and forth by the waves, and blown here and there by every wind of teaching and by the cunning and craftiness of people in their deceitful scheming."

Within a united community, our desires are fortified against the deceptive winds of false teachings and worldly influences. As we collectively strive for truth, our desires are shaped by shared values that align with God's goodness.

Community prevents isolation, a breeding ground for deception. Ecclesiastes 4:12 (NIV) underscores the power of companionship: "Though one may be overpowered, two can defend themselves. A cord of three strands is not quickly broken."

In a community that values fellowship, our desires are protected from the isolation that can make us vulnerable to deceit. The shared experiences, perspectives, and support of others provide a barrier against the deceptive influences that thrive in solitude.

The role of community and accountability in guarding against deception cannot be overstated. In a world where deceptive influences can distort our desires and lead us astray, the bonds of community become a stronghold—a place where our pursuit of goodness is fortified by collective wisdom, shared values, and the power of discernment.

Through accountability, discernment, unity, and prevention of isolation, we cultivate an environment where our desires are nurtured with truth and aligned with God's goodness. As we journey together in the pursuit of transformed desires, we find that the support of a community becomes a potent weapon against the cunning schemes of deception, guiding us toward desires that reflect the purity and authenticity of our Creator.

7.5 A Reflection of God's Family

Within the heart's battleground, where desires and influences contend, the concept of community as a reflection of God's family holds profound significance. This section explores how the bonds of community and the practice of accountability mirror the nature of God's family, fostering an environment of unity, love, and growth.

Community reflects the unity of God's family. Romans 12:5 (NIV) beautifully illustrates this truth: "so in Christ we, though many, form one body, and each member belongs to all the others."

In a community of believers, our desires are intertwined with the shared purpose of pursuing goodness and glorifying God. This spiritual kinship transcends individual desires, as we recognize that our pursuits are part of a larger tapestry woven by the hands of our Creator.

Community mirrors God's family through love in action. John 13:34-35 (NIV) captures the essence of this reflection: "A new command I give you: Love one another. As I have loved you, so you must love one another. By this everyone will know that you are my disciples, if you love one another."

Within a community, our desires are directed toward embodying the love of Christ. The practice of accountability becomes an expression of this love, as we help one another navigate the heart's battleground with grace, compassion, and a shared commitment to growth.

Community nurtures growth through discipleship. Titus 2:3-5 (NIV) speaks to the value of mentoring within God's family: "Likewise, teach the older women to be reverent in the way they live, not to be slanderers or addicted to much wine, but to teach what is good. Then they can urge the younger women to love their husbands and children, to be self-controlled and pure, to be busy at home, to be kind, and to be subject to their husbands, so that no one will malign the word of God."

In a community that values discipleship, our desires are cultivated through the guidance of seasoned believers. The practice of accountability becomes a form of spiritual mentorship, fostering growth in our desires and a deeper understanding of God's goodness.

Community reflects our shared identity in Christ. Galatians 3:28 (NIV) underscores this shared bond: "There is neither Jew nor Gentile, neither slave nor free, nor is there male and female, for you are all one in Christ Jesus."

Within a community, our desires are shaped by the realization that we are all equal members of God's family, regardless of our backgrounds or circumstances. This shared identity fuels our pursuit of goodness and unity, transcending superficial differences and aligning our desires with the values of God's kingdom.

The concept of community as a reflection of God's family holds profound implications for our pursuit of goodness. In a world where self-centered desires and divisions can fragment our sense of belonging, the bonds of community and the practice of accountability remind us that we are part of something greater—a family united by our love for God and our pursuit of His goodness.

Through unity, love, growth, discipleship, and shared identity, our desires find fertile ground within the context of God's family. As we journey together, supporting, encouraging, and sharpening one another, we discover that the practice of accountability within a community is not just a means to an end, but a reflection of the very nature of our Creator—a nature characterized by unity, love, and a shared commitment to transformation in pursuit of desires that honor and glorify Him.

7.6 Journeying Together in Pursuit of Goodness

Amidst the heart's battleground, where desires and influences vie for supremacy, the significance of journeying together in pursuit of goodness within a community cannot be overstated. This section delves into the profound impact of embarking on the transformative journey of aligning our desires with God's goodness as a united community.

Journeying together within a community provides strength in shared purpose. Ecclesiastes 4:9-10 (NIV) aptly captures this idea: "Two are better than one, because they have a good return for their labor: If either of them falls down, one can help the other up."

In a community, our desires become intertwined with the collective pursuit of goodness. The shared purpose of seeking God's best for our lives fortifies us with a sense of unity and camaraderie, enabling us to overcome obstacles and celebrate victories together.

The journey within a community is guided by the compass of accountability. Proverbs 27:17 (NIV) illustrates this guidance: "As iron sharpens iron, so one person sharpens another."

In a community that values accountability, our desires are kept on course by the input and guidance of trusted companions. Accountability ensures that our pursuit of goodness remains true to God's principles and free from the pitfalls of deception.

Journeying together fosters mutual encouragement. Hebrews 10:24-25 (NIV) urges believers to "spur one another on toward love and good deeds, not giving up meeting together, as some are in the habit of doing, but encouraging one another."

Within a supportive community, our desires are fueled by the encouragement of fellow believers. Their affirmation, support, and shared experiences inspire us to persevere, even when the challenges of the heart's battleground seem daunting.

Journeying together is enriched by shared testimonies of transformation. Revelation 12:11 (NIV) speaks to the power of testimony: "They triumphed over him by the blood of the Lamb and by the word of their testimony."

In a community, our desires are influenced by the stories of others who have undergone transformation. These testimonies offer hope, inspiration, and a tangible reminder that the pursuit of goodness leads to a life marked by God's redemptive work.

Journeying together within a community is a testimony to the transformative power of God's goodness. In a world that often isolates and divides, the bonds of community and the shared pursuit of transformed desires stand as a powerful testament to the beauty of collective transformation.

Through shared purpose, accountability, mutual encouragement, and the power of testimonies, we discover that the journey of aligning our desires with God's goodness is not solitary but communal.

As we navigate the heart's battleground alongside fellow believers, we find that the struggles and triumphs of transformation are shared experiences that bind us together. The journey within a community is a reflection of God's design for His children—a design that celebrates unity, encourages growth, and ultimately leads to desires that mirror the heart of our Creator.

Chapter 8: Seeking God's Protection

In the heart's battleground, where desires and influences clash, seeking God's protection is essential for maintaining our pursuit of goodness and safeguarding our transformed desires. This chapter delves into the significance of seeking God's protection through prayer, discernment, and a deep reliance on His guidance.

8.1 The Shield of Prayer

Amidst the tumultuous heart's battleground, where desires and influences wrestle for supremacy, the shield of prayer emerges as a vital source of protection, guarding our pursuit of goodness and nurturing our transformed desires. This section delves into the profound significance of prayer as a shield that fortifies our hearts and guides our desires.

Prayer is a refuge in the midst of confusion. Psalm 91:4 (NIV) poetically captures this reality: "He will cover you with his feathers, and under his wings you will find refuge; his faithfulness will be your shield and rampart."

In the heart's battleground, where conflicting desires and deceptive influences can cloud our judgment, prayer serves as a sanctuary of clarity. As we lay our desires before God, we invite His presence to envelope us, offering protection from the confusion that can lead us astray.

The shield of prayer aligns our desires with God's will. 1 John 5:14-15 (NIV) assures us: "This is the confidence we have in approaching God: that if we ask anything according to his will, he hears us. And if we know that he hears us—whatever we ask—we know that we have what we asked of him."

In the heart's battleground, prayer becomes a channel through which our desires are refined and shaped by God's wisdom. As we surrender our desires to His sovereign plan, our hearts become attuned to His purposes, ensuring that our pursuit of goodness is harmonious with His intentions.

The shield of prayer strengthens our resilience. Philippians 4:6-7 (NIV) offers this encouragement: "Do not be anxious about anything, but in every situation, by prayer and petition, with thanksgiving, present your requests to God. And the peace of God, which transcends all understanding, will guard your hearts and your minds in Christ Jesus."

In the heart's battleground, prayer bolsters our emotional and spiritual fortitude. Through prayer, we exchange anxiety for peace and uncertainty for assurance. This inner peace becomes a shield that guards our hearts and empowers us to navigate the challenges of the battleground with courage and determination.

The shield of prayer grants access to divine wisdom. James 1:5 (NIV) promises: "If any of you lacks wisdom, you should ask God, who gives generously to all without finding fault, and it will be given to you."

In the heart's battleground, prayer opens a channel through which we can seek God's wisdom to discern between conflicting desires and influences. As we seek His guidance through prayer, our desires are illuminated by His truth, enabling us to make decisions that honor His goodness.

The shield of prayer offers communion with God. Psalm 16:11 (NIV) celebrates this truth: "You make known to me the path of life; you will fill me with joy in your presence, with eternal pleasures at your right hand."

In the heart's battleground, prayer fosters intimacy with God. Through prayer, we encounter His presence, experience His love, and draw near to His heart. This communion becomes a shield that guards us against the lies and deceptions that seek to divert our desires away from His purposes.

The shield of prayer is not merely a defensive measure, but a transformative force within the heart's battleground. Through prayer, our desires are refined, aligned, and fortified. As we engage in heartfelt conversations with our Creator, our desires are enveloped in His wisdom, love, and protection, empowering us to pursue goodness with a steadfast heart. Ultimately, the shield of prayer is a gift that allows us to participate in the ongoing work of transformation, guiding our desires to mirror the very heart of God.

8.2 The Discerning Heart

In the heart's battleground, where desires and influences clash, the discerning heart emerges as a critical tool in seeking God's protection and maintaining alignment with His goodness. This section delves into the profound role of discernment as a shield that safeguards our desires and guides us away from deceptive influences.

The discerning heart is a compass that helps us navigate through deceptive paths. 1 John 4:1 (NIV) advises believers to "test the spirits to see whether they are from God, because many false prophets have gone out into the world."

In the heart's battleground, where desires can be easily swayed by deceptive influences, discernment serves as a filter. It enables us to differentiate between desires that are aligned with God's truth and those that are influenced by false teachings, worldly values, or self-centered motives.

The discerning heart aligns our desires with God's Word. Hebrews 4:12 (NIV) underscores the power of God's Word: "For the word of God is alive and active. Sharper than any double-edged sword, it penetrates even to dividing soul and spirit, joints and marrow; it judges the thoughts and attitudes of the heart."

In the heart's battleground, discernment is nurtured by immersing ourselves in Scripture. As we engage with God's Word, our desires are illuminated by His truth, enabling us to recognize desires that are in harmony with His character and purposes.

The discerning heart recognizes deceptive influences. Matthew 7:15 (NIV) warns against false prophets: "Watch out for false prophets. They come to you in sheep's clothing, but inwardly they are ferocious wolves."

In the heart's battleground, discernment acts as a guard against the subtle allure of deceptive influences. Through prayerful reflection and seeking the counsel of wise mentors, we develop the ability to identify desires that are shaped by deceitful ideologies, ensuring that our pursuit of goodness remains untainted.

The discerning heart cultivates wisdom. Proverbs 2:6 (NIV) affirms, "For the Lord gives wisdom; from his mouth come knowledge and understanding."

In the heart's battleground, discernment matures into wisdom through the Holy Spirit's guidance. As we surrender our desires to God's leading, our hearts are shaped by His wisdom, enabling us to make choices that align with His goodness and purposes.

The discerning heart serves as a shield of spiritual insight in the heart's battleground. Through its guidance, our desires are safeguarded from the subtle ploys of deception, ensuring that we pursue only that which honors God's truth.

As we cultivate discernment through prayer, Scripture, and a reliance on the Holy Spirit's guidance, our desires become fortified against the distractions and distortions that can lead us astray. Ultimately, the discerning heart is a shield that helps us journey confidently in pursuit of goodness, guarding our desires and guiding us toward a life that reflects the discerning and transformative character of our Creator.

8.3 Guided by God's Spirit

In the heart's battleground, where desires and influences contend, being guided by God's Spirit stands as a cornerstone in seeking His protection and nurturing transformed desires. This section explores the profound significance of relying on the Holy Spirit's guidance as a shield that directs our desires and ensures alignment with God's goodness.

Guidance by God's Spirit is a divine compass in times of uncertainty. Galatians 5:16-17 (NIV) highlights this role: "So I say, walk by the Spirit, and you will not gratify the desires of the flesh. For the flesh desires what is contrary to the Spirit, and the Spirit what is contrary to the flesh."

In the heart's battleground, where desires can waver and external influences pull us in various directions, the guidance of the Holy Spirit serves as an unerring compass. As we submit our desires to His leading, we find assurance that our pursuits are guided by His wisdom, rather than being swayed by fleeting impulses.

Being guided by God's Spirit transforms our desires through yielding. Romans 8:5-6 (NIV) describes this transformation: "Those who live according to the flesh have their minds set on what the flesh desires; but those who live in accordance with the Spirit have their minds set on what the Spirit desires. The mind governed by the flesh is death, but the mind governed by the Spirit is life and peace."

In the heart's battleground, the guidance of the Holy Spirit reshapes our desires as we yield to His influence. Through surrender, our desires are redirected toward pursuits that align with God's goodness, infusing us with life, peace, and a renewed perspective.

Guidance by God's Spirit acts as a filter for decision-making. John 16:13 (NIV) assures us of the Spirit's role: "But when he, the Spirit of truth, comes, he will guide you into all the truth. He will not speak on his own; he will speak only what he hears, and he will tell you what is yet to come."

In the heart's battleground, where choices can carry significant consequences, the Holy Spirit's guidance serves as a filter that helps us discern between desires that lead to life and those that lead to destruction. His promptings and insights provide clarity, enabling us to make decisions that are in line with God's will.

Being guided by God's Spirit empowers us to overcome desires of the flesh. Galatians 5:22-23 (NIV) lists the fruit of the Spirit, which includes self-control: "But the fruit of the Spirit is love, joy, peace, forbearance, kindness, goodness, faithfulness, gentleness and self-control. Against such things there is no law."

In the heart's battleground, where the desires of the flesh can lead us astray, the Holy Spirit equips us with self-control—a shield against impulsive and self-centered desires. His presence empowers us to choose desires that are in harmony with God's character, rather than yielding to momentary indulgences.

Being guided by God's Spirit is more than just a philosophical concept; it's a practical reality that shields us in the heart's battleground. Through His guidance, our desires are directed, transformed, filtered, and empowered. As we lean into the Holy Spirit's leading, we find a trustworthy guide who navigates us through the complexities of desires and influences, ensuring that our pursuits remain steadfastly aligned with the goodness and purpose of our Creator.

8.4 Trusting in God's Sovereignty

In the heart's battleground, where desires and influences compete, the foundation of trusting in God's sovereignty becomes an essential element in seeking His protection and nurturing transformed desires. This section delves into the profound significance of placing our trust in God's sovereignty as a shield that anchors our desires and guides us through uncertainty.

Trusting in God's sovereignty provides unwavering assurance. Proverbs 3:5-6 (NIV) captures this truth: "Trust in the Lord with all your heart and lean not on your own understanding; in all your ways submit to him, and he will make your paths straight."

In the heart's battleground, where conflicting desires and external pressures can create confusion, trusting in God's sovereignty becomes an anchor. It reassures us that, even when our desires seem at odds, He is in control and will guide our paths according to His perfect plan.

Trusting in God's sovereignty enables us to cast our anxieties on Him. 1 Peter 5:7 (NIV) encourages believers: "Cast all your anxiety on him because he cares for you."

In the heart's battleground, where desires can be accompanied by anxiety and uncertainty, trusting in God's sovereignty becomes a shield that relieves our burdens. By relinquishing our desires and concerns to His care, we find peace in the knowledge that He is working all things for our ultimate good.

Trusting in God's sovereignty aligns our desires with His purposes. Romans 8:28 (NIV) assures us: "And we know that in all things God works for the good of those who love him, who have been called according to his purpose."

In the heart's battleground, where our desires can be influenced by self-centered motives, trusting in God's sovereignty transforms our perspective. We recognize that His plans are greater than our own, and we willingly align our desires with His purposes, knowing that He is orchestrating a beautiful tapestry of goodness in our lives.

Trusting in God's sovereignty leads us to find rest in His control. Psalm 46:10 (NIV) invites us: "Be still, and know that I am God; I will be exalted among the nations, I will be exalted in the earth."

In the heart's battleground, where desires can stir restlessness and impatience, trusting in God's sovereignty becomes a shield of tranquility. We surrender our desires with the knowledge that He is the ultimate authority, and we find rest in His unchanging nature and faithful provision.

Trusting in God's sovereignty is not a passive surrender, but an active stance of faith that shields us in the heart's battleground. Through this trust, our desires are anchored, our anxieties are relieved, and our paths are directed by the hand of a sovereign Creator.

As we entrust our desires to His care, we discover a shield of steadfast faith that guides us through uncertainty, transforms our perspectives, and aligns our desires with His greater purpose. Ultimately, trusting in God's sovereignty enables us to navigate the complexities of the heart's battleground with a heart that is secure, confident, and at peace in His unshakeable control.

8.5 Walking in the Light

Amid the heart's battleground, where desires and influences vie for prominence, the principle of walking in the light emerges as a guiding light in seeking God's protection and nurturing transformed desires. This section delves into the profound significance of walking in the light as a shield that dispels darkness, safeguards our desires, and guides us on a path of goodness.

Walking in the light involves embracing truth and transparency. 1 John 1:5-7 (NIV) beautifully captures this essence: "This is the message we have heard from him and declare to you: God is light; in him there is no darkness at all. If we claim to have fellowship with him and yet walk in the darkness, we lie and do not live out the truth. But if we walk in the light, as he is in the light, we have fellowship with one another, and the blood of Jesus, his Son, purifies us from all sin."

In the heart's battleground, where desires can be influenced by hidden motives and deceptive intentions, walking in the light becomes a shield that exposes darkness. By embracing truth and transparency, our desires are brought into the open, allowing God's light to purify and guide us toward paths of righteousness.

Walking in the light involves choosing holiness over compromise. Ephesians 5:8-10 (NIV) exhorts believers: "For you were once darkness, but now you are light in the Lord. Live as children of light (for the fruit of the light consists in all goodness, righteousness and truth) and find out what pleases the Lord."

In the heart's battleground, where desires can tempt us to compromise our values, walking in the light becomes a shield that steers us away from moral compromise. By intentionally choosing the path of holiness, our desires are safeguarded from influences that would lead us away from God's goodness.

Walking in the light involves renewing the mind. Romans 12:2 (NIV) encourages transformation through mind renewal: "Do not conform to the pattern of this world, but be transformed by the renewing of your mind. Then you will be able to test and approve what God's will is—his good, pleasing and perfect will."

In the heart's battleground, where desires can be clouded by worldly influences and distorted perspectives, walking in the light becomes a shield that renews our minds. Through God's Word and the guidance of the Holy Spirit, our desires are shaped by a renewed understanding of His will, enabling us to discern what is truly good and pleasing to Him.

Walking in the light involves exposing hidden motives. Hebrews 4:13 (NIV) reveals the depth of God's knowledge: "Nothing in all creation is hidden from God's sight. Everything is uncovered and laid bare before the eyes of him to whom we must give account."

In the heart's battleground, where desires can be driven by hidden agendas and selfish motives, walking in the light becomes a shield that exposes the true nature of our desires. As we invite God's penetrating gaze into the depths of our hearts, our motives are purified and aligned with His pure and righteous intentions.

Walking in the light is more than a metaphor; it's a transformative principle that guides us through the heart's battleground. Through truth, holiness, mind renewal, and the exposure of hidden motives, our desires are illuminated by God's light, ensuring that we navigate the complexities of life with a heart that is aligned with His goodness.

As we choose the path of light over darkness, our desires find protection from the distortions of the world, and we embark on a journey of transformation that leads to desires that mirror the very heart of our Creator. Ultimately, walking in the light becomes a shield that guides us toward a life marked by authenticity, righteousness, and the pursuit of lasting goodness.

8.6 Fortified by God's Protection

In the heart's battleground, where desires and influences collide, the concept of being fortified by God's protection emerges as a stronghold in seeking His guidance and nurturing transformed desires. This section delves into the profound significance of God's protective care as a shield that strengthens our resolve, guards our desires, and empowers us to walk in alignment with His goodness.

Being fortified by God's protection provides divine strength amidst human weakness. 2 Corinthians 12:9-10 (NIV) illuminates this truth: "But he said to me, 'My grace is sufficient for you, for my power is made perfect in weakness.' Therefore, I will boast all the more gladly about my weaknesses, so that Christ's power may rest on me."

In the heart's battleground, where our desires can sometimes be influenced by our own limitations and vulnerabilities, God's protection becomes a shield that bolsters us. His strength prevails in our weakness, empowering us to pursue desires that honor Him, even when our own strength falters.

Being fortified by God's protection guards our desires from harm. Psalm 121:7-8 (NIV) declares: "The Lord will keep you from all harm—he will watch over your life; the Lord will watch over your coming and going both now and forevermore."

In the heart's battleground, where desires can be exposed to harmful influences and potential derailment, God's protection serves as a shield that watches over us. His care safeguards our desires from being tainted by the world's corrosive influences, guiding us toward paths that lead to lasting goodness.

Being fortified by God's protection empowers us to stand firm. Ephesians 6:10-11 (NIV) exhorts believers: "Finally, be strong in the Lord and in his mighty power. Put on the full armor of God, so that you can take your stand against the devil's schemes."

In the heart's battleground, where desires can face opposition and spiritual battles, God's protection becomes a shield of empowerment. As we put on the armor of God—truth, righteousness, faith, and more—we are equipped to stand firm against the forces that seek to divert our desires away from God's goodness.

Being fortified by God's protection becomes a lifeline in times of temptation. 1 Corinthians 10:13 (NIV) offers assurance: "No temptation has overtaken you except what is common to mankind. And God is faithful; he will not let you be tempted beyond what you can bear. But when you are tempted, he will also provide a way out so that you can endure it."

In the heart's battleground, where desires can face alluring temptations, God's protection acts as a shield that offers a way of escape. His faithfulness ensures that we are not overwhelmed by temptations that would compromise our desires; instead, He provides a way for us to endure and remain steadfast.

Being fortified by God's protection is an assurance that we are not left defenseless in the heart's battleground. Through His strength, care, empowerment, and guidance, our desires are shielded from harm, opposition, and temptation.

As we lean into His protective embrace, our desires find a secure foundation that enables us to pursue goodness with unwavering confidence. Ultimately, being fortified by God's protection leads us to navigate the complexities of life's battleground with a heart that is rooted in His steadfast love, guiding us toward desires that reflect His transforming and redemptive grace.

Chapter 9: Journal Prompts

Journaling is a powerful tool that allows you to reflect, process, and apply the insights you've gained in your journey of guarding your heart. These journal prompts are designed to help you delve deeper into the concepts explored in this devotional and to encourage personal growth and transformation.

9.1 Reflecting on Your Heart's Desires

- Take a moment to reflect on your current desires. What are the primary desires that shape your thoughts and actions?

- Consider whether your desires are aligned with God's goodness and purposes. Are there desires that need to be realigned?

- Write down three desires that you believe are in harmony with God's will. Reflect on how pursuing these desires can bring honor to Him.

9.2 Embracing God's Protection

- Describe a recent situation where you felt the need for God's protection in navigating conflicting desires. How did you seek His guidance and protection?

- Share a personal experience where you felt God's protective care shielding you from harmful influences. How did His protection impact your desires and decisions?

- Consider a desire that you're struggling to guard against worldly influences. Write a prayer asking for God's protection and guidance in keeping that desire aligned with His goodness.

9.3 Applying Discernment and Wisdom

- Recall a time when you faced conflicting desires and needed discernment. How did you seek God's wisdom to make the right choice? What was the outcome?

- Write about a desire that initially seemed good but turned out to be deceptive in nature. How can you apply discernment to similar desires in the future?

- Share an instance when God's wisdom guided you away from a desire that could have led to compromise. How did this experience impact your view of discernment and its role in guarding your heart?

9.4 Trusting in God's Sovereignty

- Reflect on a desire that you've struggled to entrust to God's sovereignty. What steps can you take to relinquish control and trust in His perfect plan?

- Describe a time when you felt a deep sense of peace by trusting in God's sovereignty amidst conflicting desires. How can you cultivate that trust more consistently?

- Write a prayer of surrender, entrusting all your desires to God's sovereign care. Express your willingness to align your desires with His greater purpose.

9.5 Walking in the Light of Truth

- Consider a desire that you've hesitated to bring into the light due to shame or fear. How can you take steps to confess and address this desire in God's presence?

- Write about a situation where walking in the light led to greater clarity and alignment with God's goodness. How can you intentionally cultivate transparency in your desires moving forward?

- Reflect on how walking in the light can transform your desires. What practices or habits can you adopt to ensure that your desires are consistently exposed to God's truth?

9.6 Fortifying Your Heart Through Prayer

- Share a recent experience where prayer served as a shield in the face of conflicting desires. How did prayer help you overcome challenges and maintain alignment with God's goodness?

- Write a prayer asking for God's protection and guidance in a specific area of your life where desires are in tension. Include a request for the Holy Spirit's discernment.

- Consider how the shield of prayer has fortified your heart in your journey of guarding your desires. Describe how your prayer life has evolved and its impact on your desires.

Reflect on your journey of exploring and applying the principles of guarding your heart throughout this devotional. How have your perspectives on desires, protection, discernment, sovereignty, walking in the light, and prayer evolved?

In your journal, summarize your key takeaways from each chapter and how they have influenced your desires and decision-making. Express your gratitude for the insights gained and your commitment to continue cultivating a heart that is aligned with God's goodness.

As you conclude this devotional, remember that your journey of guarding your heart is ongoing. Use this journal as a tool to revisit these concepts, track your growth, and seek God's guidance in the ongoing transformation of your desires.

Chapter 10: Social Posts

Sharing your insights and reflections on social media is a wonderful way to inspire and encourage others in their own journeys of guarding their hearts. These social media posts are crafted to help you share key takeaways from each chapter of the devotional.

10.1 Reflecting on Desires

� "Our desires shape our thoughts and actions. Let's pause and reflect on the desires that drive us. Are they aligned with God's goodness and purpose? Let's pursue desires that honor Him! �� #GuardingMyHeart #DesiresAligned"

10.2 Embracing Divine Protection

� "Amidst life's battles, I'm learning to embrace divine protection. God's shield guards my desires and guides me on paths of goodness. His strength prevails in my weakness, and His care keeps me safe. �� #GodsProtection #FortifiedByGrace"

10.3 Seeking Discernment

� "In the heart's crossroads, discernment is my guiding light. Seeking God's wisdom helps me distinguish between desires that lead to life and those that deceive. Let's cultivate discerning hearts together! �� #SeekingWisdom #DesiresInAlignment"

10.4 Trusting in His Plan

� "Trusting in God's sovereignty is my anchor in uncertainty. I'm letting go and trusting that His plans are greater than mine. His ways are perfect, and His protection guides my desires. �� #TrustingGod #WalkingByFaith"

10.5 Walking in His Light

� "Walking in the light exposes darkness in my heart's desires. Transparency and truth are my allies in this journey. Let's shine the light of God's truth on our desires and walk in His radiant goodness! �� #WalkingInTheLight #HeartTransparency"

10.6 Fortified by Prayer

� "Prayer is my shield against conflicting desires and challenges. It's through prayer that I find strength, discernment, and alignment with God's will. Let's build a fortress of prayer around our hearts! �� #PrayerWarrior #GuardedHeart"

10.7 Personal Growth Journey

� "This devotional journey has transformed the way I view my desires. With each chapter, I've learned to guard my heart, seek discernment, trust in God's sovereignty, and walk in His light. Grateful for growth and excited for the future! �� #PersonalGrowth #JourneyOfFaith"

Feel free to adapt and personalize these social media posts to reflect your own experiences and insights. Sharing your journey with others can inspire them to embark on their own path of guarding their hearts and pursuing a life of transformed desires in alignment with God's goodness.

Chapter 11: Prayer

Prayer is a powerful avenue through which we communicate with God, express our desires, and seek His guidance. As we conclude this devotional, let's delve into the significance of prayer in guarding our hearts and nurturing transformed desires.

11.1 A Conversation with the Creator

Prayer is more than a monologue; it's a conversation with the Creator. Psalm 145:18 (NIV) reminds us, "The Lord is near to all who call on him, to all who call on him in truth."

In this sacred dialogue, we lay our desires before God, sharing our hopes, dreams, and challenges. As we open our hearts in vulnerability, we invite God to shape our desires in alignment with His goodness.

11.2 Surrender and Submission

Prayer is an act of surrender and submission. Matthew 26:39 (NIV) portrays Jesus' example: "Going a little farther, he fell with his face to the ground and prayed, 'My Father, if it is possible, may this cup be taken from me. Yet not as I will, but as you will.'"

In prayer, we surrender our desires to God's perfect will. We acknowledge that His ways are higher than ours and that His plans are ultimately for our good. Through submission, our desires are refined and reshaped by His wisdom.

11.3 Seeking God's Wisdom

Prayer is a means of seeking God's wisdom. James 1:5 (NIV) assures us, "If any of you lacks wisdom, you should ask God, who gives generously to all without finding fault, and it will be given to you."

In prayer, we seek discernment and understanding as we navigate conflicting desires. God's wisdom illuminates our choices, guiding us toward desires that reflect His character and purposes.

11.4 Expressing Gratitude

Prayer is a way of expressing gratitude. Philippians 4:6 (NIV) advises, "Do not be anxious about anything, but in every situation, by prayer and petition, with thanksgiving, present your requests to God."

In our conversations with God, we express gratitude for His protective care, guidance, and the transformation of our desires. Gratitude deepens our connection with Him and fosters a heart that is attuned to His goodness.

11.5 Building Intimacy

Prayer builds intimacy with God. Psalm 139:1-2 (NIV) captures His knowledge of us: "You have searched me, Lord, and you know me. You know when I sit and when I rise; you perceive my thoughts from afar."

Through prayer, we invite God into the depths of our hearts and desires. As we share our hopes and struggles, our intimacy with Him deepens, shaping our desires to mirror His heart.

11.6 A Lifeline in Challenges

Prayer is a lifeline in challenges. Psalm 34:17 (NIV) assures us, "The righteous cry out, and the Lord hears them; he delivers them from all their troubles."

In the midst of conflicting desires and the trials of life, prayer becomes our refuge. We lean on God's strength and protection, finding solace in the knowledge that He hears our cries and cares for our desires.

Let's Pray

Dear Heavenly Father,

As I come before You in prayer, my heart is filled with gratitude for the journey I've embarked on through this devotional. You have revealed the profound truth of guarding my heart and nurturing transformed desires. With each chapter, You have illuminated the path that leads to alignment with Your goodness.

Lord, I acknowledge that my desires shape my thoughts, actions, and the course of my life. I am reminded of the importance of examining these desires and ensuring that they are in harmony with Your will. Help me to be intentional about pursuing desires that honor You, drawing me closer to Your purpose for me.

I am humbled by the promise of Your protection. Your shield guards me from harmful influences and empowers me to stand strong even in the face of challenges. May Your strength be made perfect in my weakness, and may Your protective care guide my desires toward paths of righteousness.

Give me discernment, O God. Open my eyes to recognize the deceptive nature of certain desires and lead me to choose those that reflect Your truth and goodness. I seek Your wisdom as I navigate the complexities of life, allowing Your Word to be a lamp to my feet and a light to my path.

Lord, I place my trust in Your sovereignty. I surrender my desires to Your perfect plan, knowing that Your ways are higher than mine. Help me to release control and to find peace in the knowledge that You are working all things together for my good.

Walking in Your light has brought clarity and transformation to my desires. As I expose my heart to Your truth and transparency, may Your light dispel any darkness within me. Let transparency be my guide as I seek to honor You in all aspects of my life.

In prayer, I find strength, wisdom, and intimacy with You. Thank You for being a refuge in times of challenge and temptation. I lean on Your protective embrace and trust that You will provide a way of escape from every temptation that comes my way.

As I conclude this devotional journey, Lord, I commit to keeping this conversation alive. May my prayer be a continuous dialogue with You—a lifeline that guards my heart, shapes my desires, and leads me ever closer to Your heart.

Thank You, Heavenly Father, for the transformative insights I've gained and the growth I've experienced. May my desires be a reflection of Your goodness, and may my life be a testimony to the power of guarding my heart in alignment with You.

In the name of Jesus, I pray - Amen.

As we conclude this devotional, remember that prayer is a continual conversation—a lifeline that sustains us in the heart's battleground. Through prayer, our desires are refined, realigned, and transformed by the One who knows us intimately.

Let your prayer be a constant refrain, guiding you in guarding your heart and nurturing desires that honor God's goodness. May your journey of seeking His protection, discernment, and guidance through prayer lead you to a life marked by transformed desires and a heart that reflects His radiant love.

Chapter 12: Conclusion

As we bring this transformative journey to a close, let's reflect on the path we've traversed and the lessons we've embraced. The journey of guarding the heart and nurturing transformed desires is a lifelong pursuit—an adventure that shapes our character, influences our choices, and aligns our hearts with the goodness of our Creator.

Throughout this devotional, we've explored the profound significance of our desires and the role they play in shaping our lives. We've delved into the heart's battleground, where unseen battles are fought, and choices are made. We've learned the importance of guarding against deception, seeking discernment, and walking in the light of truth.

We've journeyed through the landscapes of transformed desires—desires that delight in the Lord, find contentment in His provision, and reflect His goodness. We've discovered the power of renewal, the beauty of transparency, and the strength of unity within a community of like-hearted individuals.

Our path has led us to seek God's protection, to trust in His sovereignty, and to fortify our hearts through prayer. Through every twist and turn, we've witnessed the transformation of desires, the refining of intentions, and the cultivation of a heart that beats in rhythm with God's heart.

As we conclude this journey, let's remember that this is not a destination but a beginning—a beginning of a life characterized by guarding the heart, seeking transformed desires, and pursuing goodness. The insights gained, the truths internalized, and the wisdom acquired are the stepping stones that guide us forward.

May the lessons learned within these pages become the guiding principles of our lives. May we be empowered to navigate life's complexities with discernment, to honor God in our desires, and to extend His love to those around us.

As we step away from these words and embark on the journey ahead, let's carry with us the echoes of transformed desires. Let's remember that our hearts are a canvas where God's goodness is painted in the hues of our choices. May we walk forward with hearts that reflect His light and love, that guard against deception, and that nurture desires aligned with His purposes.

The journey continues—one step at a time, one choice after another. Through the peaks and valleys, the victories and challenges, may we be unwavering in our commitment to guarding our hearts and embracing transformed desires. And as we journey, let's extend our hands to others, inviting them to embark on this adventure with us—a journey that leads to a heart overflowing with the goodness and grace of our Creator.

With gratitude for the lessons learned and the transformation experienced, let's embrace the call to live lives that honor God through the desires we pursue and the choices we make.

May this journey be a testament to the power of guarding the heart, nurturing transformed desires, and walking in the footsteps of the One who leads us on this extraordinary adventure.

In the name of Jesus, our Guide and Redeemer, we say, "Amen."

ACTION:

1.) Extract the positive ideas that align with you

2.) Apply them to your life with consistency

3.) Enjoy the benefits you receive :)

RELATED CONTENT

You will become what you consume and surround yourself with.

If you like this content please connect with our other books, posts, and videos. *Search for "BGodInspired"*. If we have something you need, we believe you will find it at the point it's valuable in your life.

More importantly that connecting with BGodInspired... we hope you connect directly with God.

Prayer is a powerful tool that connects us with God.

Prayer is our communication with our Creator - allowing us to express our desires, concerns, and gratitude. Here are some benefits of prayer:

Connection with God: Prayer establishes a direct line of communication with God, enabling us to connect with Him on a personal and intimate level. It deepens our relationship with Him and strengthens our faith.

Source of Comfort: In times of distress, prayer provides solace and comfort. It allows us to cast our burdens upon God, knowing that He cares for us and desires to bring us peace in the midst of turmoil.

Guidance and Wisdom: Through prayer, we seek God's guidance and wisdom. It opens our hearts and minds to receive His direction, helping us make decisions that align with His will and bring peace to our lives.

Transformation of Heart: Prayer has the power to transform our hearts and minds. As we pour out our concerns, confess our sins, and seek God's forgiveness, prayer brings about spiritual healing and renewal, leading to inner peace.

Surrender and Trust: Prayer is an act of surrendering our will to God and placing our trust in Him. It helps us let go of control and rely on His sovereignty, leading to a sense of peace that comes from knowing He is in control.

Don't over complicate it - just talk to God.

Don't miss out!

Visit the website below and you can sign up to receive emails whenever BGodInspired publishes a new book. There's no charge and no obligation.

https://books2read.com/r/B-A-XYAY-GDDSC

BOOKS 2 READ

Connecting independent readers to independent writers.

Also by BGodInspired

Civil Rights

Foundation of Freedom - The Divine Call

Prophets of Justice - Faith in Action

Struggles and Sacrifices - Overcoming Adversity

The Power of Unity - Building Bridges

Short Bible Answer

Short Bible Answer: Forgiveness

Short Bible Answers: Patience

Short Bible Study

Short Bible Study: Exodus 14:14

Short Bible Study: Ezekiel 16:49

Short Bible Study: Proverbs 4:23

Short Bible Study: 1 Thessalonians 5:18

Short Bible Study: Romans 3:23

Short Bible Study: Matthew 6:34

Short Bible Study: Matthew 5:14

Short Bible Study: Mark 12:31

Short Bible Study: Philippians 4:13

Short Bible Study: Philippians 4:6

Standalone

Guarding Your Heart

About the Author

BGodInspired is an inclusive place... where we want to help you find inner joy... where we want you to better understand yourself... where we want to provide you the motivation to get more from life... as only God can provide it.

We provide short messages so they are easy to consume.

We believe in Inclusion: One God, multiple religions. One Jesus with two core commandments: Love God and Love Others (no exceptions). One Spirit that connects us all, many perspectives.

www.ingramcontent.com/pod-product-compliance
Lightning Source LLC
LaVergne TN
LVHW091109150826
845673LV00002B/758

* 9 7 9 8 2 2 3 7 6 4 5 8 8 *